The Beast in the Café

Coffee with Don Pedro
Steve Tanham

A writer watches the world go by over a quiet coffee on a sunny afternoon. The arrival of an insistent Pomeranian and his mysterious owner is about to turn his world upside down as everyday objects become the tools that lead first to knowledge, then to the glimmering of understanding...

Steve Tanham tells the story of one man's encounter with an unusual approach to a spiritual journey and an unorthodox teacher.

Published by Silent Eye Press

Copyright©Steve Tanham 2015

ISBN-13: 978-1910478134 (Silent Eye Press)

ISBN-10: 191047813X

The Beast in the Café

Coffee with Don Pedro

Steve Tanham

The Beast in the Café was originally published in serial form on the website of The Silent Eye.
thesilenteye.co.uk

The Silent Eye is an international School of Consciousness, founded by Steve Tanham, offering a correspondence course and online teaching seeking to bring awareness of the magic inherent in everyday life.

Contents

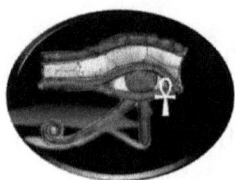

I - IX
The Beast in the Café

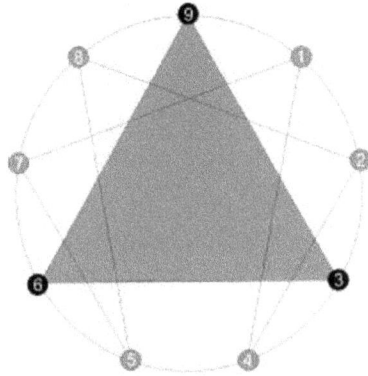

I

It was a grey winter day, the kind that resonates with the eternally stretching mud sands of Morecambe Bay, on whose Northern reaches, and to the South of Lakeland, sits Grange-over-Sands. The wind cut you like a knife and seemed to be sweeping right off the dark sea.

The Sunrise Café is slightly inland, at the far end of the little town, but even its usually sheltered terrace was chilled beyond endurance. I entered the café, mumbled my order through frozen lips, and waited, snug in the warmth, knowing what was to come. The large and steaming mug of happiness materialised before me, and I threw in a few of the tiny but complementary marshmallows that adorn the counter, before, looking like one facing death, I turned to begin my self-imposed ordeal.

Clutching my coffee-to-stay, I passed a bemused Maria Angelo, who was serving an elderly couple at a table by the door, and went out of the café's warm and chintzy interior to sit in the arctic. I picked as unobtrusive a seat as I could and sat down, pretending to look at the few shops. There's not a lot see in this part of the town. I let my fingers absorb the warmth of the mug while it lasted, and tried to clear my mind in a long-practiced, but usually doomed, attempt at presence.

"You not smoking," said a gruff voice, from behind me.

In my haste to sit and drink, I had not noticed the large figure in the corner. He also held, with fingers half-covered by partial woollen mittens, a hot mug, the steam rising to his corpulent face. He was a bull of a man, with shoulders nearly as wide as his body. Next to him, standing on the cold concrete of the café's terrace, and looking quizzically at me, was a fox.

"He not a fox," said my interrogator, with a wry smile. "He

Pomeranian . . ."

My fingers clutched at the hot mug for mental security. The beast of a man smiled, cruelly, at my discomfort. "You not smoking," he said again, as my mouth opened in mute response, and I contemplated the demise of my normally orderly Thursday morning.

I coughed to provide some time to think. Was he threatening me? Some sort of psycho?

"I don't smoke," I said in a flat tone, not particularly wanting to provoke, but defending my freedom to do what the hell I liked, even if it was odd.

"Hah! He said, with a triumphant laughing snarl. "So why you out here, freezing nuts off?" He slapped his thigh as he spoke. I thought about his words and realised that he wasn't English. Italian possibly, or Spanish? I sipped my coffee and tried to summon my James Bond face. I don't really have one, but the idea can be reassuring, sometimes . . .

I would try an assault of my own and frighten him off.

"I'm doing a Gurdjieff exercise in presence," I said.

"Oiff!" said the fox.

My antagonist thumped the table. Maria Angelo, passing by the door, interpreted this as him wanting something, and came to stand facing him. Grinning like a giant bear, he stared back at her. After a twenty second stand-off, she gave up on his silence, bent forward to re-arrange his cup and dripping coffee spoon, and left, slamming the café door on her way into the warm interior.

"Pedro, think Gurdjieff rubbish!" said the beast, delighted with the turn of events. I was surprised at two things – that the fox, now revealed as a talking Pomeranian called Pedro, was so well educated; and, secondly, that my attempt to blind my opponent with intellect had so miserably failed. I sipped my coffee and stared at him in silence.

After a while his grinning face rose, came to tower over me and said,

"Finish coffee. There is colder café down by shore . . ."

II

I didn't follow him to the shore café. I can hear my inner sighing as I relate this to you now. In retrospect, the leap was too much, too soon. Have you ever found that? That something or someone knocks on your door and invites you into a new life . . . and we're often too daunted to take it. We spend days, even weeks, thinking about how such a gateway might 'look', only to turn our back on it when it arrives. There is a curious human trait of being able to ask for something, even though we can't actually describe it . . . I suspect that it's the nature of knowledge: we seek to know something, which, by definition, we don't know – and yet we know what we want to know! It implies that there is actually a form of Knowing that precedes the knowledge. Curious . . .

It was a further two months before I saw Don Pedro, again. I was sitting outside in the unseasonal early April warmth at the Sunrise Tea Rooms quietly sipping my second latte, and scribbling furiously in my notebook. The Land of the Exiles workshop was only two weeks away, and I had left the presentations till the last minute. Some years I begin with the talks, some years I begin with the scripts. This year had definitely been script-led. The voices of the crew in the crashed spaceship "The Hawk" had grown and grown in intensity in the act of their creation. What had seemed very daunting at the outset (could we really use a sci-fi basis for something sacred?) had gathered its own momentum as an inner intelligence smiled and muttered, "Oh ye of little faith . . . "

In the distance I could hear a faint, "Oiff". I froze. It came again, slightly nearer. "Oiff, Oiff".

I put down the pen and looked for the source of the sound. I have only ever known one dog that made that bark and, sure enough, he had just turned the corner of the café's patio garden and was headed my way!

Pedro, not to be confused with his master, Don Pedro.

I looked at the grinning (yes grinning) dog at my feet as he wagged his bushy, golden tail and smiled. You think a dog can't smile?

Within seconds, Pedro, this strange dog I hardly knew was standing on my knee and laughing at me.

"Pedro, like you . . ." came the dreaded voice from my blind side. The huge bulk of Don Pedro materialised behind me, laughing. He took the seat opposite me. "You very comfortable" he said, nodding, in answer to his own question. "Warmer than last time . . ."

I started to answer, but my antagonist had spotted Maria Angelo, the Spanish waitress and raised an urgent finger. She froze when she saw him.

"We take two coffee," and then he paused, a twinkle in his demonic eye, "Please . . ."

My existing cup was still half-full, but I didn't argue. Pedro the Foxy Pomeranian, wagged his tail in approval at my decision not to run away. He made a small "Oiff" sound and jumped down to lie at my feet, his job done for the day. I was secured under the overbearing presence of his master.

Determined to say nothing, I let the new coffees arrive. Maria Angelo looked at me with concern, the beautiful brown saucers of her eyes asking me, mentally – "You want I should call manager?" I smiled up at her in reassurance. I wasn't frightened of the Beast, but he was unnerving to be near, the feeling of discomfort wasn't painful. It was more a sense of being vulnerable without any fear attached to it.

"You comfortable now," said Don Pedro, again. It wasn't a question. "Comfort important if you want to sleep . . ." That inner sound of stretched string had begun again. He took a huge gulp of steaming coffee, as if to punctuate the sentiment, then stood up. Pedro, looking irritated that the event was over so quickly, jumped off my warm knee and down to stand by Don Pedro.

"I like man with freezing nuts," he grunted. "He had courage." He took a second swig of piping liquid and drained the coffee. "Is he gone? Perhaps he find us next time?"

With that, Don Pedro turned away and walked out of the café. Pedro took one final, and slightly sad, look at me, then turned to follow.

I sat, looking at the cup full of coffee, the cup drained of coffee and the silence around the table.

And wondered . . .

III

There comes a point in any true search when there is that temptation to give up. If the quest has been authentically begun, such a moment seems, in retrospect, to be a test. It is like a line of dots, seen on the level of their own 'plane', in which one after the other comes at you, obscuring the incoming stream.

Now, imagine that you rise above the next incoming dot and see it from above. There, finally, you see many of them coming at you, and that all the dots are really part of a line and that the line has direction and purpose – and you at the end of it. It is actually part of the language of Being, and you have the choice of being an unwitting receiver of dots or a driver of lines. Either way, they're coming for you. . . It's just a matter of which way you're facing . . .

"Perhaps you find us, next time?" Don Pedro had said.

I remember that, at the time he said it, I had viewed it as an easy task – more test of willingness than of finding. I would go to the shore café, whose image had formed in my mind on the first day we had met. He would be there, smiling up at my change of status from arrogant know-it-all, to seeker of what he might just know . . .

But, now, a week later, he wasn't there. The shore café was closed for a refit. Apparently their musical oven had begun to overpower the conversations of the clients, and Jenny, the joint owner, had finally agreed to part with it. But, I knew of another café, close by and on the edge of the park with the mandarin ducks. With a psychological sense of "why are you doing this" ringing in my head, I set off for the second destination, with no clear hope of finding him. How much this reflects life, I thought. We travel as though we have a destination and yet we don't. We are just caught in the flow, as though we entered a river at birth, and presume that the passing landscape on the banks is due to our efforts or that we have any control over it, at all . . .

In dark mood, I crossed from the esplanade, under the railway line, and walked up through the car park. I arrived at the Pantry café's old stone steps and entered its lower floor, where a few tables are always set for coffee and cakes. There was no sign of Don Pedro, no jumping foxy dog to tell me that another meeting between us was imminent. I confess to feeling a little despairing.

One of the faces of despair is that disconnect between what you know you felt when you set off, and where you find yourself, now. Like an idea of how you will end your life, versus the gentle stroke of reality, passed to you by a loving friend, that you may not end up there at all. We all believe that we have an infinite number of moves left to us, whereas . . .

My darkening reverie was interrupted by an "Erff" – Not an "Oiff" as before; but I knew the tone of that bark. I turned to see Pedro the foxy dog wagging his tail in the doorway. I called, softly, to him, hoping that his arrival was a harbinger of that of Don Pedro, his master. No such luck. "Erff," said my golden companion, "Erff". Stubbornly, he waited at the door for me. The café owner gave me a suspicious look.

"No dogs in here, mate," he said, hesitating to give me the coffee and cake menu.

"Sorry," I muttered, getting up to join the beckoning dog. "Back later . . ."

Pedro led me back under the railway line, and we turned left along the seafront, headed for the station. I followed him diligently as he trotted onto the platform nearest the sea. He looked across the tracks and my eyes followed his gaze. Don Pedro was standing on a train that was about to depart. I could clearly see him through the window. I started forward, the habitual tension forming at something not quite grasped. Pedro barked again, as though I should magically fly over the tracks and enter the carriage. With a mounting sense of uncertainty, I realised that the train was actually moving. The bulky figure of Don Pedro, seen through the glass, began to slide to my right as the train set off for Arnside. Involuntarily, I held out my hand and shouted something. What about Pedro the dog, and what about me?

The part of the carriage where Don Pedro was standing reached one of the large iron pillars that grace the far end of Southbound platform. And suddenly he disappeared.

I realised I was feeling sick. Something was happening to my perception that had never happened before. The train completed its exit and Pedro and I stood, staring at the departing carriage, host to the disappearance of Pedro's master. "Rish," muttered the Pomeranian, looking up at me and wagging his tail. "Rish."

I stared, in an arc, between the dog and the place where Don Pedro had briefly been. I had no idea of what to do next. If the dog had crossed over to the far platform, and then both of them had departed, it would have been a simple case of Don Pedro's bad manners. But the dog looked entirely at home, rishing at me. I could swear he was grinning . . .

The tap on my shoulder, made me cry out, involuntarily. In panic, I turned to see a grinning Don Pedro. "Good trick, eh?" he chortled, bending his bulk down in a surprisingly fluid movement and patting Pedro. "You think me on train," he chortled, "But I just walk along far side . . ." He laughed at my bemusement. "Life like that," he said, speaking in a different tone, directly into my mute silence.

"All day we stare at trains, when what we want see is beyond both train windows . . ."

Pedro rubbed himself against my legs, smiling.

Don Pedro couldn't stop laughing at me. There were tears of mirth forming in his, suddenly kind, eyes.

"Coffee?" he asked. He took my arm and pushed us towards the station's small buffet. "I buy . . ."

IV

"Oiff."

The sound in the distance made me smile. I could feel Pedro racing towards me, happy little Pomeranian that he was. I didn't turn until the last minute, then, spun in my chair just as the foxy dog leapt into my lap. His master, Don Pedro, wasn't far behind, bowling along the promenade. For all his bulk, the man could move.

"Pedro say you never buy him coffee!" said Don Pedro, dropping his mass into the second of the outdoor plastic chairs around the small table.

"He doesn't drink coffee," I responded, preparing to be bemused.

"That not the point," huffed Don Pedro, and said no more to relieve the logical tension.

"How about a sausage and some water," I answered, warily.

"Hah!" he answered with a raised chin. "Think you buy him off so easily . . ." But I couldn't help noticing the edges of a slight grin around his huge mouth. I was finally getting to know this alarming and enigmatic figure. His ability to get me off guard and keep me there was . . . well, different. He seemed to induce a strange sense of heightened consciousness that I had, initially, taken to be fear on my part – but it wasn't, it was a kind of induced alertness. I was learning that Don Pedro had absolutely no qualms about doing anything. Yet, he always seemed to get away with it, as though the rest of the world around him and his victims were asleep . . . apart from Maria Angelo, the waitress at the Sunrise Tea Rooms, who now, spotting her long-standing adversary, charged up to our table with a snarled, "Yes!"

"He buying us coffee," said Don Pedro, pointing a thick,

butcher's finger at me. Maria turned to face me.

"Yes!" she said, in a slightly muted second volley, to show that she understood that this madman had imposed himself on both our lives.

Feeling impetuous, I took and kissed her hand. She stood back and stared at me, for once, speechless.

"Forgive me," I said softly into her incredulous eyes. "For all that you suffer at the hands of those on this table. Please know that we are truly grateful."

Maria backed away into the café, muttering in Spanish. Don Pedro smacked the table.

"Remarkable," he bellowed. "You stop time . . ."

"I did what?" I said.

"You break flow of what expected and stopped time . . ." His eyes were full of glee. He reached into his overstuffed waistcoat – his only outer garment – and took out an old golden pocket watch. He pointed to the Schaeffer fountain pen that I use to make my presentation notes when I'm feeling creative. I had taken to bringing it, and a leather bound notebook, to the café. It had been a present from my father to mark the occasion when I managed to get into one of the local grammar schools. It is a cherished object.

"I have valued object from my Father, too," Don Pedro said. He placed the watch next to my pen, narrowly avoiding the arrival of Maria and two large lattes, which were slapped down onto the unyielding metal surface, causing them both to spill. Don Pedro took a napkin and carefully mopped up the coffee spill, chuckling quietly in his mirth.

"She angry with you!" he chortled.

"Me!" I blurted, reaching for the overfull coffee cup – a subconscious, retaliatory gesture on Maria's part, I decided.

Ignoring my protestations, Don Pedro pushed his gold watch towards me. "I carry this all my life," he explained. "My father and his father before that, too." He beamed at me. "Your pen precious, too?"

I told him of its origin and why it was special to me. He nodded as I spoke.

"We come to identify with such things."

"Identify?"

"Yes, identity of self become embedded in objects – no use," he said with a surprising air of gentleness.

He gulped his coffee down, slurping it. I marvelled at the asbestos lining of his mouth. Pedro stood up on my lap as though preparing to go.

Don Pedro rose. "Toilet," he said, pointing to the back of the tea rooms and weaving his bulk through the tables.

"Oiff!" said Pedro, jumping down and following his master.

I sipped my coffee, looking down at the two fine objects before me. I picked up the gold pocket watch and held it. You could almost read the vibrations of the man in the shining and worn metal. I waited . . . and waited . . . and waited.

Half an hour later, I picked up both the valuables and paid the bill. The toilet was empty, of course.

I left the Sunrise Café quietly, feeling the weight of the two objects of desire in my pockets as though they were burning holes in my garments.

V

We had been talking and drinking coffee in the Sunrise Café for an hour. Now quite familiar with each other, Don Pedro and I spoke freely about our views on life and our favourite bits of philosophy.

Today, he was feeling garrulous. He was seldom so, and I took full advantage of it. The day was very hot and Pedro, the Pomeranian, was sheltering under the table. We had been talking about the effort needed to "stop time" as he put it. This term had crept into our conversation during a previous encounter, and had assumed an importance in our discussions. I didn't, for a minute, think that we were capable of actually stopping time, but that was the corresponding subjective feeling that went with a successful attempt.

"Like seeing behind moment," Don Pedro said. "Like pulling back ordinary life as though screen!" He was now shaking his giant head vigorously, and I marvelled at his enthusiasm. I liked the analogy. We had discussed the effort required to conjure such a moment, believing that this was the start of any truly 'magical' event.

"Need extraordinary effort to pull back screen of ordinary life," he said, grinning at his verbal cleverness and moving his huge arms around, in a large tearing motion, thereby endangering the lives of the nearby customers in the garden terrace.

"Don Pedro, are we talking about effort in the sense of Will?" I asked, curious about how he viewed this key ingredient to 'stopping time'.

He returned to his coffee, taking a giant slurp and banging the mug back on the table. Maria Angelo came into view and he fixed her with his predatory gaze. She spotted this and curled around our table in a wide arc, like a bull fighter, sizing up the adversary. He nodded his head, and she did, too, as though they were acting out some weird dance. The effect on those present was electric. Don Pedro broke the spell with a rasped, "I pay!" and the café returned to normal, as she hurried off to complete his request.

I doubted that anyone present could have described the moment in any detail, yet they were all mesmerised by it at the time. I was beginning to see his point – that there was a class of events that could be injected into 'ordinary life' that changed our consciousness in a very special way.

The bill was duly brought, and Don Pedro, paid – unusual in itself. That done, he stood up and motioned that I should join him. "We go walk," he said with enthusiasm.

"Yes, I'd like that," I replied, picking up the backpack with which I usually travel. I long ago ran out of the capacity for jacket pockets to contain all my paraphernalia, and there's usually my iPad in there, too, so that I can write on the hoof.

All this adds weight, of course, so after a mile or so in the hot sun, walking along the road out of Grange in an Easterly direction, I was beginning to wonder how long this 'walk' would be.

"Do we have a destination, Don Pedro?" I asked, with a small hint of concern in my voice.

"Very close – we go where I live!"

This was news to me. I had never thought to ask where the man and dog lived. Mollified by this, for no logical reason, I trudge along behind the twin Pedros for another half mile before asking again. The path had completely given way to a fast country road along which we were now striding at a considerable pace. I was getting hot and some of the discomfort edged its way into my voice.

"How much further, Don Pedro?" I ventured.

"Nearly there . . . just around corner," he pointed ahead, to no apparent destination that I could see.

Half an hour later, we arrived in Lindale. I knew I looked hot and somewhat irritated by the turn of events. Despite his bulk, he did not, and Pedro was content to trot along beside us both, dancing in the sunshine. We came to a small cottage and he patted his waistcoat pocket. Looking bemused.

"What's wrong, Don Pedro?" I asked warily, beginning to suspect that this was no ordinary mishap.

"Left keys in café . . ." The sadness on his face looked genuine. "So sorry – we need go back!"

"Go back!" I blurted out. "On foot, in this heat?"

He nodded at me, sadly. "Sorry," he said. But no sooner had he made the apology than he and foxy Pedro were trotting along at the same pace they had maintained since leaving Grange on the first leg. I trudged along behind them both, feeling strangely abused by the turn of events.

An hour later, we arrived back at the Sunrise Café. Don Pedro cornered Maria Angelo as she came out the café's interior. "You have my keys!" he barked.

"You crazy man, you know I have no keys of yours!" She flicked him with her tea towel, but smiled as she disappeared back into the interior.

"Getting old," he said, looking defeated and patting his waistcoat. From three feet behind him, I could hear the jangling of keys. "Found!" he said, triumphantly, showing them off to the startled customers in the late afternoon sun.

I crumpled into a chair, getting my breath and trying to make sense of the events. As usual with Don Pedro, I felt that I had no control of any of the events that had befallen me. He leaned over my tired form. "Suppose you not walking back with us?" he asked innocently. Not waiting for my negative response, he whistled at foxy Pedro, who had disappeared off in the direction of the doggy water that the café leaves outside on hot days. Soon the two of them were trundling off down the high street, at the same speed that they had maintained for the whole walk.

"He tell you about effort," asked Maria Angelo, taking my coffee order and using the first soft voice I had ever heard her use.

"Yes," I answered meekly.

"He tell you about special effort that teaches stopping time?"

"Yes," I said, feeling my lesson unfold, but surprised that it was coming from his antagonist, who was nodding at me, sympathetically.

"He know he not leave keys," she said, continuing to look at me with kindness.

"Then what was the point?" I asked, in an irritated voice that I was immediately ashamed of.

"He has all that and walk home, again," she said with a flicker of humour, in her lovely brown eyes.

"That is special effort . . ." With that she moved away from me in an arc, as she had done with Don Pedro, but including me, this time, in her strange dance movement.

The coffee, when it came, was apparently on the house.

VI

When I next met Don Pedro, it was one of those dark and overcast summer days for which Cumbria is famous. Unusually, he was at the Sunrise Café ahead of me, and occupied a table for four, in contrast to our usual table for two – tucked in the corner, at my insistence – so that we could keep as low a profile as possible. I tried not to register my irritation that he had changed our seating arrangements as I approached him. I had spotted something red on the table, and now I saw that he had before him an old, red jumper and that he was picking at a woollen thread. I stared at it. Its colour reminded me of a childhood woollen my grandmother had knitted for me. I had been very fond of it. When, finally, it became too small, she sat me on the settee next to her and I marvelled as she unpicked all the wool, ending up with a new-looking ball that could be re-used. I had never forgotten the transformation of seeming complexity to simple thread.

"Morning, Don Pedro!" I intoned, as cheerily as possible. I didn't want my irritation at the changed seating to show, as he would seize on it as an example of what he called "ego behaviour". As I sat down I noticed two things: Pedro the foxy dog was missing; and there was no coffee on the table-top. "I busy," he said, not looking up. "You buying coffee . . ."

I was well used to such opening gambits on his part. Maria Angelo appeared in timely fashion and took me completely by surprise by planting a kiss on my head.

"He not knit you jumper," she said, the brief kiss imparted. "Two coffees, usual?"

I was getting faster at spotting their hidden chemistry; in fact, I was beginning to suspect that they operated a bit of a double act . . . I caught the briefest flicker of a smile on the corners of his large but enigmatic mouth. He saw that I had, and chortled at me, "She stop time . . . see that?" I had been expecting that. "Yes," I replied, smiling and feeling the resentment about the seating evaporate. "She did," I said, "and very pleasant it was, too . . ."

The little chuckle said it all. "She more clever than look," he said, the smile broadening. I watched him unravel the small woollen garment, determined not to say anything. I was not going to fall into one of his traps and blurt out something obvious.

"You not talk much, today?" he asked, exasperatingly.

"I watch and learn," I said waving irritated hands over his work.

"You mad at change of table?" he opined, accurately. Damn this man! How could he unpick my feelings and thoughts as accurately as he was unpicking the red wool, which was now being wound, expertly, into a large ball on the table in front of me. Maria Angelo arrived with the coffees. She lowered them gently, not spilling them as she had on previous occasions – in what I now suspected were a series of staged tableaux. Something in my gut shifted slightly as I realised that it was quite possible that I had been the target of their attentions all along. Within me, a fight was brewing. I watched as the protagonists took their stations. In the green corner was a deeper, feeling person, amused, delighted and slightly flattered to be the focus of this rare attention, but knowing there would be a price – a commitment. In the red corner was an irritated person, used to getting his own way and superior to the little games they were obviously playing with my intellect . . . "He not knitting you jumper," she said again, in a flat tone that was irritatingly devoid of answers.

I sucked in a deep breath, suppressing the desire to ask, loudly, what the hell he was doing. Don Pedro continued unpicking the red woollen; the rewound ball getting bigger and bigger. Maria Angelo just stood there, so close to me that I could feel the warmth from her body on this rather chilly day. The juxtaposition of disproportionate tensions made me issue a small, involuntary moan. Don Pedro nodded his head, slightly, finishing the ball of red wool, which he knotted off, expertly. Maria Angelo, still silent, picked up my spoon and stirred my coffee, in the habitual way she had seen me do. I stared at her delicate fingers, seeming to lose myself in the gentle swirls of pale froth they were generating. A sense of utter silence descended on me. I felt like a patient on an operating table with the anaesthetic beginning to take effect. I was aware only of the fingers of my waitress, gently stirring the drink, in an uncharacteristic action. The silent but gentle intrusion was almost palpable. Neither of them said a thing.

The distant "Oiff" brought me back to consciousness. Dazed, I was aware of the arrival of Pedro. He brushed passed my right leg in greeting. I looked up from my reverie to see Don Pedro getting up from the table, taking a final sip from his coffee as he did so.

He nodded to me, smiled and left, taking a bouncing Pedro with him.

The stirring of coffee had stopped, but Maria Angelo remained by my side. Her eyes were looking down at the tightly wound ball of red wool in the middle of the table.

"You like colour?" she asked, softly.

"That colour, yes." My reply was simple and truthful. "It reminds me of my childhood."

"Yes," she said with a sigh. Then she smiled and her voice became bright, "Mine was blue . . ."

I reached to pick up the woollen ball, weighing it in my hand. It was heavier than I had expected.

"Not jumper anymore . . ." she said.

"The jumper was too small, anyway . . ." I said, responding unconsciously. I didn't know on what level we were having this conversation, but it was one of the strangest experiences I had ever known.

"That why he did it," she said. It was practically a whisper. "You need new garment . . . need to find bigger garment at end of thread."

I twisted the ball of wool, trying to find how Don Pedro had knotted off the final strands of wool. Nothing was visible save a near perfect sphere.

"Took me a while, too," she said, kissing my head, lightly, again, and leaving.

VII

I was slightly late in arriving at the Sunrise Café the day after Don Pedro had carried out his curious actions with the child's red jumper. As I strode, hurriedly, up the main street, I was scanning ahead for signs of Pedro – my little foxy friend, who seemed to act as my guide; but neither he nor Don Pedro, his master, were there. I dropped into our usual seat and looked up to see Maria Angelo arriving with my coffee. "You late . . ." she said in a matter of fact voice that would have carried irritation in other circumstances but, this time, didn't. "Road works on the A590," I muttered, lamely, looking at the single coffee. "He's not coming?" My voice carried the sense of disappointment I felt. I could feel myself dropping into that passive state of dependency that I hated. My happiness belonged to me, I mused without effect.

There was silence, and I looked up into her beautiful eyes. She smiled.

"You want he do all the work?" The question was expressed simply and with candour.

I started to speak, but she moved her eyes sideways in the manner I had sometimes seen her use when she wanted to move on, quickly.

"I brought bill," she said. "Now going off-shift . . . check and pay counter, inside." With that, she jammed the small folded chit under my coffee saucer and turned to go. I looked up, somewhat bewildered, at her departing back. She must have felt my gaze and turned around. She walked back to me and planted one of her gentle kisses on my head. "Enjoy coffee while hot," she chuckled. "You unravel start of thread?"

It had taken me a while, but I had finally located the practically invisible knot that Don Pedro had used to secure the ball of red wool. I nodded in response to her question.

"Good," she said, reaching into her pocket and taking out a plaited section of wool. She placed it next to my coffee, turned and left.

I had an ominous feeling that life was happening somewhere else; and that I had been invited . . . but had, so far, failed to arrive . . .

For a few minutes, I contemplated this strange sensation, holding it in my consciousness and letting it unravel and reveal itself in the way that Don Pedro and I had started to discuss at one of our earlier meetings. The sense of something happening was palpable – yet, here I was, sipping coffee in a café devoid of the two people who were rapidly turning life into magic.

I picked up the platted section of wool. There were three colours – 'my' red, and two more threads, one of blue, the other, orange. My heart began to race, slightly, as I considered the blue. Maria Angelo had said that her ball of wool had been blue . . . so that must mean that the orange was Don Pedro's. Three threads, interwoven . . .

Something drew my attention to the scrunched up bill, jammed under the saucer. I picked it up and unfolded it. It was hand-written, instead of the café's usual printed till receipt.

In blue letters the top line read: 'Coffee on Maria'. Beneath that, in orange letters, were written the words: 'Can't always be so easy. Now, must go Lobo for a change.'

I stared at the twin sets of letters. They had been written by two different hands – obviously Don Pedro and Maria Angelo's. But what was the message? Were they saying that our small but magical meetings were at an end? I looked again at the platted wool. No, that second object was there to encourage me . . . I had not been abandoned at this café . . . this easy café, came the thought, unbidden.

I sipped the last of my coffee, the two objects of my

morning lesson in front of me.

Lobo, I thought. I knew that word. With a flash, it came – it was Spanish for wolf.

Wolf, wolf, wolf . . . and then something turned in my head. There was a wolf connection, locally. A little way further up the coast, near Flookborough, was a headland that jutted out into the sea. Its name was Humphrey Head. It was a nature reserve but had a footpath around its perimeter which allowed unparalleled views from its heights into the turbulent seas of Morecambe Bay. Seized with a certainty that also carried urgency, I put down my coffee cup and headed for the car.

Lobo, I thought, climbing into the driver's seat, Lobo! Humphrey Head was, in local legend, the place where the last wolf in England was shot. I smiled at their irony, and gunned the engine into life, laughing. I didn't want to be late for my own execution . . .

VIII

As I left the café, I felt a sense of great urgency. The journey to the large car park in Grange over Sands takes you over an open crossing of the main Lancaster to Barrow line. I was so lost in my thoughts that I did not see the train until the last minute, dancing, mute and apologetic out of its way with seconds to spare. The shining and deadly bulk flashed past me at speed, hypnotising me with its power of life and death – and my proximity to the latter . . .

As I stood, breathlessly watching the speeding train vanish along the curve of the track towards Barrow, I thought how apt a metaphor it was to our lives. We assume we are always a long way from death – yet here, in a second now vanished into time, I had come so close that I could taste it.

Shaken, and somewhat humbled by the experience, I got into the car and drove the few miles westward to Humphrey Head. The headland juts out Southwards into Morecambe Bay, yet it stands very much apart from the rest of the landscape. From the ground it can look high and forbidding, yet I knew from a much earlier visit, that it was accessible from the high sheep pasture on its upper flank.

I parked the car at the entrance to the salt flats and looked up at the sheer mass of it. As I raised my vision, I thought I heard a small "Oiff" in the far distance. I listened hard for the sound to come again, but there was nothing more. Was I on a wild goose chase? Would I find myself alone at the top, staring into imaginings of my own creation?

The path begins with a steep curl that leaves you pointed at the peak. From here it is a more or less straight slog of about fifteen minutes to reach the rocky plateau that is the extended peak of the Head. As I climbed I noticed two mature lambs, recently sheared, enjoying the sunny weather. They didn't seem disturbed by my puffing progress and seemed content with their summer pasture. For a second I thought about how I had seemed to hear Pedro the Pomeranian from down below. It was a trivial thought, but I wondered if he was loose in the meadow – and if so could be at risk of being shot by a local farmer?

I continued to climb, eventually reaching the peak of the headland. The central path crosses up the spine of the promontory and the ground falls away steeply to the right side, revealing hidden nooks and crannies that lie on the very edge of a steep and deadly drop.

Eventually, I stood on the very highest point and scanned the land on either side. My spirits fell as I saw that I was alone up there. My febrile imagination had, once again, led me astray. Don Pedro was probably off on one of his crazy walks. Maria Angelo would be looking after her mother . . .

There is a single tree that marks the highest level. Over its life it has been battered and blown by extreme winds – but it still flourishes up here. I stood by it and looked down at the empty slope that descended, steeply, towards the sea on the far side.

This time, the sound of Pedro's "Oiff" was unmistakable. I looked around, scanning the little hillocks and valleys to find him, my heart racing. But he was nowhere to be seen. A last stage in this mad chase? But that had been his bark, so Don Pedro, at least, was here with his dog. Like a mad thing, I ran over the rocky outcrops, searching them out and feeling ridiculously joyful.

On the third attempt, I found them. They were sitting on a tartan blanket, with a red and white gingham picnic cloth spread out on the grass, in a hollow behind a group of rocks that formed a natural wind break. Don Pedro smiled up at me, pushing a cheese-filled piece of baguette into his large mouth. Pedro smiled up at me, too – in his amazing, doggy way. Maria Angeles continued to look down at the flask of coffee from which she was pouring out three small cups.

"The little wolf arrives, and has earned his new name . . ." she said, looking up at me with teasing eyes. "And just in time for his coffee, after all . . ." She let the sentence hang in the breeze. I took in the scene. It had all the hallmarks of a dream. The three figures, seated at picnic as though it were the most normal thing in the world. Becoming conscious of my hammering heart, I drew in a breath to steady myself and speak, but Maria Angelo uncurled her ballerina's body and approached me, holding up a finger to my lips. She pressed it gently to the flesh in a gesture that could not be misinterpreted; tapping it, again, as she drew me to sit down with them on the blanket. Silence.

Don Pedro finished chewing his cheese and bread. "Some things not so simple . . . not come to us . . . have to be hunted by us," he said, looking intently into my eyes. He leaned towards me and tapped three fingers on the top of my head. "Not only from head," he said, smiling. "From heart . . . Lobo understand?" I had not noticed Maria Angeles shifting her position, but as Don Pedro said the word, "heart" I felt her hand come to rest over mine.

Don Pedro leaned towards me. "Takes effort," he said, removing his spread fingers from my head. Maria Angeles' warm hand did not move. "But not just from head," he continued. "Head must be guided by heart . . ."

They continued eating. I felt my consciousness slipping into a state different from any I had known before. Strange and yet totally at home with itself . . . filled with a certainty, a trust and a knowing that something very real was happening.

"You hungry now?" Don Pedro asked.

I nodded, not sure if the prohibition on speaking had ended. But I risked it.

"Yes," I answered softly, feeling it to be right.

"Good, then eat – don't speak!"

They fed me royally. As I finished my impromptu lunch, they began to clear the things around me.

Don Pedro spoke as he pulled the blanket from under me, "You stay here one hour . . . then go and look for the sea." He pointed in the direction of the bay, down the way I had looked in despair when I thought they had never been here. I nodded my assent. The calm sense of different purpose filled me; I had no desire to leave this spot.

They left, Pedro barking me an "Oiff" as he topped the crest of the hill and disappeared.

An hour later, I walked, slowly, down to the far side of the headland, placing its massive presence behind me as I faced the sands. I remembered from my earlier glance that the tide had been far out. I took off my shoes and walked on the edge of a water-filled channel at the start of the beach. I looked out into the distance.

At the edge of my vision, the tide had turned and the blue and white horses were racing in to meet me.

IX

I didn't see them again for the next few days. I had decided that their teaching method involved the maximum amount of spontaneity. With that in mind, I reasoned, there was no need to tell them when I was next visiting the Sunrise Café – I would just turn up; but the difference would be that I would be mentally and emotionally ready for that encounter.

I wanted to ask Don Pedro where he learned his almost magical craft. It now seemed obvious that Maria Angelo had, somewhere amidst his near-constant provoking of her working life, become one of his 'students' in that strange school of what one could only call, 'the inner life'. The existence of such a method reminded me of what I had read about the ancient Shamans, but he might simply have derived it himself. Besides, no-one in their right mind would expect a Shaman to be living and teaching in Grange over Sands! He was an unlikely teacher, his bulk at odds with his vast energy. I resolved to ask him at least some of these questions as I strode up the main street from the car park and over the brow of the hill towards the café. The summer day was warm, with a clear, blue sky. It was a day to feel good about life .

Maria Angeles was serving him his breakfast. I could see boiled eggs on the table, together with his usual mug of steaming coffee. Pedro the Pomeranian gave his customary 'Oiff' bark when he saw me, and rushed to greet me, doing his best to trip me up with his living coils of foxy golden-orange around my ankles.

"Morning Don Pedro," I said, dropping into my seat. I turned to greet Maria Angeles, who was smiling at me with great warmth. "Morning, Maria Angeles," I said, in a softer tone, looking into the pools of her brown eyes. There was a growing bond between us, but I knew it was more to do with shared student-hood than anything else.

Don Pedro looked up at Maria Angeles.

"He take eggs, too."

He smiled as he said it, and she did her curly walk away from the table, fixing me in an intense way with her eyes. I could feel that strange shifting feeling in my gut as she did this. This was different from their technique of 'stopping the world'; it was something that put you into a different receptive space. Her departing body folded through the doorway and I turned to look at Don Pedro, who was holding his spoon over one of his boiled eggs.

"You fond of her?" he asked, slyly.

"Yes," I replied, honestly.

"Can't have – she mine. . ." He brought the spoon down onto the remaining egg, smashing its domed upper surface to create a precise, brutal and circular dent. Something in the action drew my attention and held it on the now-cracked egg. The 'shifted' feeling in my gut had changed to one of great tension. I drew in a breath to voice some protest, but could think of none. Instead, I let out the hot air in a gentle and wordless stream.

"Good," said my tormentor, clearing the new hatch into his egg, and dipping a toast 'soldier' into the runny golden delights beyond.

"We all have egg – we all are eggs," he said, with a twinkle in his eye. "Egg stops us seeing what IS!" He drew out the word into a hiss, then he said, "What is egg?"

He put his spoon into the egg and transferred a large portion of its interior into his mouth with relish and said through the food, "Something wonderful inside . . ." he gave me his most devious look as he spoke. He watched to see if the sentiment had registered on my dull consciousness. I was struggling – did he mean the wonderful taste of the soft boiled egg?

"One word," he said, holding up a single finger and taking another mouthful. "You give me one word only, show you understand..." and then he winked at me – something he had never done before and which I found strange and disconcerting. "And then we continue . . ."

I stared at him as he poured the remainder of the hot coffee into his asbestos mouth, wiped his lips with the napkin, and stood up. Maria Angeles arrived with my breakfast and studied the two of us, intently, weighing up the situation. She put her hand on my shoulder as she laid out the twin egg cups, toast and hot coffee. Don Pedro leaned down to stroke his dog, Pedro, then dog and master left without a further word.

Maria Angeles took something from her pocket and leaned over towards my eggs, now sitting proud in their cups. There was a silver flash as her sharp knife cut though the top of the first one, leaving me with a surgically perfect exposed ring of white and gold.

"No need for brutality," she said, conspiratorially, in my right ear. "Precision just as good! Women understand such things . . ." With that she left. I sipped my coffee and stared at the precision wound in front of me, wondering.

After a while I leaned forward to pick up the neatly severed top of my egg. Experimentally, I tried putting it back on to its former body. It fitted perfectly. I sat back and considered the repair – it was almost seamless, and contrasted darkly with the remembered, mangled remains of Don Pedro's egg, now long cleared away.

One word, he had said, ominously – implying that we were going no further until he had it . . .

Shaking my head, I tucked into my breakfast . . . a man had to eat, after all.

X –XVII
Coffee with Don Pedro

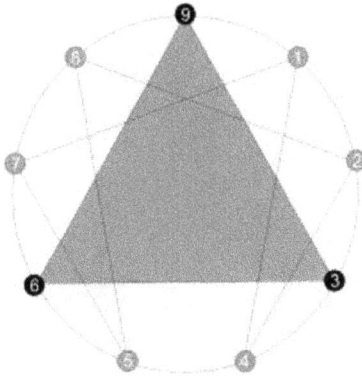

X

For a week, I worried at his question: "One word," he had said. "One word show you understand!" I had visited Grange several times since our last encounter. I hoped the landscape would jog the memory of events, causing them to take on a new order of meaning.

It was obvious that Don Pedro – and Maria Angelo – were connected in some union of the mind or spirit -call it what you will . . . they seemed to have set themselves the task of seeing if I was made of the 'right stuff' to join them. It was all very esoteric, but I had nothing against that. I had trained as a computer scientist way back, but, although I liked and respected science, I no longer felt it had all the answers.

The problem was that science had formed its own paradigms long ago, like a tree of logic built upon a few foundations. You could no longer challenge – or even usefully discuss – those foundations or you would run straight into a brick wall of prejudice. Science was brilliant at dealing with the material realm, and, in truth, in the years of its origins had cleared out so much dross that was holding humanity back. But, when it came to consciousness it either deferred to the psychologists or pointed to the huge gap between interstellar billiard balls and the mind; and added that it would bridge the gap, one day.

Science operated in a worldview where the 'out there' held precedence. Everything in science had to be built from that disconnected palette or it wasn't real, including ourselves – despite the gaps bigger than anything else in physics.

Mysticism, of all flavours, began with an alternate view, building on the premise that our relationship with the 'out there' was fundamental to our – and its – existence. Such an arena of continuity had been envisioned as far back as the Druids, and probably much further. But science couldn't find the derided mysterious vibration that connected all in such a scheme and so dismissed it as fantasy . . .

With these thoughts in mind, I began to review what had happened to me at the hands of Don Pedro, Maria Angelo, and occasionally, the Pomeranian, Pedro. To start with, I had suffered the transition of smart philosophical know-it-all to amazed-of-Grange. What had begun as an engaging conversation in the freezing exterior of the Sunrise Café had turned into an ingress into my consciousness by two people who possessed what I can only describe as, a different energy. During our last encounter, I had thought of them as possibly modern Shamans, but I wasn't sure that they fitted any label. They seemed to operate at a tricky level of consciousness which gave them a greater perspective on the now and it possibilities . . . Dull and everyday moments suddenly came alive in their hands. The most extraordinary experiences emerged from coffee cups and eggs!

I thought about the eggs. Don Pedro's smashed with brutality, Maria Angelo's cut with absolute precision. The tops removed in what had to be symbolic gestures of great import. Both actions had left me speechless.

Why eggs?

I changed my position on the park bench, watched the Mandarin ducks and sipped my flask of coffee. I was irritated at my lack of progress and had denied myself cafés until I solved it. I thought about how Don Pedro had reached across and smashed the top of my egg, after first telling me that I couldn't have his woman – Maria Angelo, though I did not have any designs on her of that nature.

Just the memory of it hurt . . . hurt . . . suddenly, I could see a glimmer of meaning in what they had done. They had set out to produce a set of feelings in me – and had succeeded. I thought about this for a while. Those feelings had changed my relationship to the event in question – and to them, for a second or two, until I got my equilibrium back, and reverted to a state of real watching, instead of responding. Anyone can be rude to another, but that wasn't the point of what they had done, I had never seen them waste energy on such things, though Don Pedro had appeared to be merciless to Maria Angelo until I saw the game they were playing with my consciousness. . . drawing me into their little drama . . . acting their parts.

I looked across at a fellow park-dweller, who was eating a packed lunch. I chuckled at the synchronicity as he took out a boiled egg and began to peel it. The man was of indeterminate age, completely bald but of youthful complexion. Despite it being summer he wore a long khaki rain mac. As I watched him, his careful handling of the egg drew me in, and, moments later, I found myself looking into his kindly eyes.

"I love eggs, don't you?" he asked.

I coughed in embarrassment and stuttered a reply, "Sorry, didn't mean to stare at you. Yes, I like eggs too – especially like that: cold and hard-boiled."

He seemed pleased at the interaction; nodded and resumed his lunch. I had better be careful, I thought, staring at people like that, my ego had taken a battering of late and I didn't want to invite more of the same.

My ego . . . I caught myself running the word through my mind. Ego, sounding just like 'egg'.

Something shifted in my mind and I sipped my coffee. My companion had finished his lunch, packed away its remains in an ex-army canvas shoulder bag and was leaving. As he passed me, he smiled and extended his hand.

"George," he said. "George Dixter." I part stood to take the proffered hand then sat down again, carefully, not wanting to spill the last of the coffee.

"I've seen you around, it's a small town." His smile widened, but I was getting that buzzing in the head and couldn't reply.

Looking intently at me, he said, "I'm sure we'll meet again." With that he strode off, leaving me sipping the last of the coffee and wondering about Grange-over-mystery. Then I realised that I hadn't even told him my name, and he hadn't reacted to that, at all.

I returned to my thoughts. I had a mental lead. Egg to ego. The notion that made sense of their seeming act of café brutality the previous week.

It was my turn to pack up my bits. I left the park sporting a grin. Time to find them, I thought. Time to risk that one word that was a key to our future . . .

XI

I hurried up the hill towards the higher part of Grange in which the Sunrise Café is located. Even from a distance, I could see Don Pedro's bulk as I got closer. I was bursting with the 'one word' answer and eager to test it. He was sitting at our usual table, but, strangely, with his back to my direction of travel. Normally he would be facing my arrival. Something inside me chuckled at the notion. I could see a blaze of orangey gold fringed on his knees. Pedro the Pomeranian was sitting on his knee. As I drew closer, time seemed to change its very quality, as though each step took exponentially longer. In this totally focussed state, I watched a slowed down, but infinitely graceful Maria Angelo approach the table with two mugs of steaming coffee on a tray. I watched as she placed them before him, slowly turning to look at me – and smiling, warmly.

I realised I had stopped moving. I was standing just behind Don Pedro in total stillness. The only contact between us was through Maria Angelo's soft brown eyes.

"Are you going to stay outside the circle forever?"

He had not moved but his voice had lost its customary gruffness, there was gentleness there. What did he expect? He was sitting in my chair . . . . With a start, I realised the fixed nature of the sentiment 'my chair' – how totally apt; how symbolic of the unmoving nature of our consciousness, our fixed views on reality. Feeling a strange sense of what I can only call empowerment, I walked past his turned back and around the table. I did not look at him as I took my new seat. Maria Angelo followed me with her soft but intense gaze.

Then I looked up into the eyes of them both . . .

"Reaction," I said, softly, into the empty space between the three of us.

Then time and space exploded. Don Pedro leaned forward and thumped the table so hard it made the two coffee cups bounce . . . but nothing spilled.

"He does it!" he cried, in jubilation, then, with eyes that fixed me like a snake. "Why?"

I gathered my thoughts, carefully weighing the possibilities, selecting those of the fewest words.

"Because what we are does not react . . ."

There was the sense of liquid flowing in the space between us. I looked up into Maria Angelo's eyes just before she bent forward and hugged me. At the same time, Pedro became a golden arrow that ended up on my knee. Don Pedro said nothing, but was smiling, too.

The tableau that was the four of us lapsed into total silence. I remember noting that we seemed invisible to those around us in the sunny café. The lack of noise was profound. Don Pedro began sipping his coffee, and gestured that I should have mine. I took the second cup without questioning it.

"And so, we see that what we are is hidden in what appears to be," he took his customary huge swig of hot coffee. "And therefore we must explore this that is not, to find out why we are locked into its viewpoint . . ." I realised with a start that he had spoken in utterly fluent English for the first time. Why the devil . . . .

I started to speak, but Maria Angelo placed a gentle finger over my lips. She picked up my coffee and sipped it, then passed it back to me in a gesture of instruction.

As the coffee drained, I watched the two of them hug in what appeared as celebration. Then, Don Pedro rose to leave, calling Pedro off my knee. The golden one turned to look at me just before he scampered off with a customary 'Oiff'. Maria Angelo returned to her duties in the café.

I was alone again. Enjoying the sheer presence of the

moment, I drained my cup, slowly, realising, with a smile, that I had never ordered it . . .

XII

I felt elated, three days later, as I strode into the Sunrise Café. I wondered what form my "acceptance" into their strange company would take? Smiling to myself; and proudly reliving my moment of triumph the previous week, I was surprised to find the front garden of the café empty. I looked around – there were people inside the building but none out here . . . which was unusual for a sunny day.

I sat back and enjoyed the silence. Maria Angelo would be along shortly, I was sure. I waited, and waited . . . but no-one came. Had I been abandoned, so soon after my induction!? I could feel the ire rising in my guts. How dare they . . . and then I began to watch myself, seeing the part of me that was doing precisely what I had stumbled upon as the key word for entry: Reaction. At the thought of not being special, I had dropped straight back into reactive mode, again.

I felt quite light-headed at the speed with which this had taken over my consciousness. I stood up and walked around the café garden, thinking what a strange sight I must look from the interior. But no-one was watching my inner struggle. I turned to face the exit, wondering if this was the end of the lesson, if I should accept that sometimes there could only be myself at such moments.

And there he was.

Pedro, the golden Pomeranian, was standing on the pavement next to the café, not even looking at me, just turned away, nonchalantly, as though waiting for me to get there.

I voiced a gentle, "Hello, Pedro" and he turned, made his customary "Oiff" greeting, and brushed around my ankles. Then, he set off back down the street. For a second, I watched him leave, then a rude voice in my head muttered, you're supposed to follow him, dummy! And, dropping the thinking mind that had so recently plagued me, I did.

For the first few minutes, he padded through the main streets of Grange, occasionally turning to check that I was following. He was embarrassingly faster than me, and I had to maintain a near trot to keep up with him. Soon, we had left Grange behind, and were walking on the edge of the main road out of town and towards Lindale. I vividly remembered the day that Don Pedro had duped me into walking to what he said was his village in the hot sunshine, taking me there – then back, under the pretext that he had left his keys in the café. I looked at the golden dog trotting along in front of me. This didn't have the feel of a similar event, but only time – and an hour's walk – would tell. I thought of that day and my use of the word duped to describe the nature of the event. Don Pedro had arranged things so that he and his golden companion, now before, me, were the only ones who had to walk the final leg, back to his home. Thinking this, again, I felt slightly disingenuous at my reaction. Never in my life had I felt so much inner alchemy going on!

And so, we trotted, Pedro and I, as cars swept past us on the busy road without a footpath. I mused on that – there was a way through, here, but it didn't belong to pedestrians! I thought of the symbology, the traveller on the sole path, with just a dog for company, but maybe that was too far-fetched . . .

Finally, we reached the outskirts of Lindale, and Pedro took a sharp left onto a footpath that ran along a field and over the back of the village. This was a deviation from the route that Don Pedro had taken me on my previous visit. Perhaps we had been nowhere near his real home – always assuming that was our destination this time?

The path dropped down into a hollow and before me were a few old farm buildings. Pedro speeded up and disappeared behind one of them. I followed, eager not to lose my only guide.

I couldn't help it, the tiny caravan before me made me giggle. It was at once the cutest object I had ever seen and also the most ridiculous dwelling! Looking like something out of a child's book, it dominated the space on which it sat with its oddness.

Pedro was nowhere to be seen, so I explored this strange space. The tiny caravan was parked near to a wall, in a small space which had been turned into a lovely little garden that somehow matched the caravan's nature.

My gaze was led from a beautiful border of flowers, up the dry stone wall to a trellis, where abundant roses grew against the sky. For a moment I stopped in my search for my absent teacher and simply let myself Be in this strange, ethereal place.

There was a cough from a point to the right of me, and the spell was broken. I turned to see three figures sitting at a table which was jammed, impossibly, between the far part of the curving stone wall, and the tiny caravan.

One was Don Pedro, the other, now on his knee and looking very pleased with himself, was Pedro, intently licking his master's chin; and the third was a man I recognised from my strange visit to the park in Grange, when I had eaten my boiled eggs alongside a stranger who had done the same, then introduced himself.

"Tea, for change?" asked Don Pedro.

"Love to," said George Dixter, sitting on the small, folding camping chair next to the encroaching bulk of the larger man. Pedro seemed content with Don Pedro's chin.

The three of them looked up at me with a quizzical expression.

"Hmm?" asked Don Pedro, waving the teapot at me . . . "Tea?"

XIII

"Trust," said the new man – George Dixter. "In the end it has to start with trust . . ." He let the words tail off, and took another bit of the cold pizza.

Don Pedro stared, apologetically, at the food his companion was consuming voraciously.

"You longer than expected," he said, as though exasperated. "Have to eat something!"

I sat back in my tiny camping chair, clutched my tea, and felt it rock backwards, taking my centre of gravity to the point where another slight movement would take me over and down, to connect with either the grass or the old tire of the tiny caravan that was being portrayed as Don Pedro's home. A certain lightness of being was welling up inside me – a feeling that wasn't just feeling, that threatened to overwhelm, or even shatter my everyday existence. I wanted to laugh, but laughter wouldn't do justice to whatever was unfolding in my consciousness.

Don Pedro was talking. I had drifted away for a second. "Not good with tea, but you want?" I looked up at him to see he was patiently holding out a thin slice of the cold pizza that he had extracted from a take-away box. Embedded in the idea of trust, I took it from him and inserted it after the next sip of the hot tea. He was right, it was dreadful, but I chewed it, gratefully, anyway.

"Food very important," said Don Pedro, watching me chew, absently. "We need be conscious to the eating; need see right back to the making of the food, and before that, to the life that gave itself so we can sit here and chew . . . our lives like food. We need learn to give!"

I suddenly felt slightly ashamed of my absent chewing,

and noticed how their actions had driven away any semblance of everyday and mundane consciousness. They both appeared to be adept at this. I thought of Maria Angeles, and how it appeared they were grooming her to join them in whatever over-arching plan they had.

"Trust developing well," said Don Pedro, looking into my eyes more gently that I ever seen him do before. I chewed some more, trying to think back along the chain of giving that led to the thin slice of pizza being consumed by the automated machine that my mouth usually was. How special we viewed ourselves to be – hardly connected with the world we had conquered in this age of supreme reason.

Dixter sat forward in his tiny chair. He was still wearing the old beige raincoat I had seen him in, two weeks ago, in the park with the ducks. I wondered if he ever took it off.

"This is what's left of my farm," he said. "You are welcome here any time you wish." He waved his arm as though mocking his kingdom. "Don Pedro lives here, in this tiny caravan – with Pedro, of course . . . this is not a trick."

His voice was precise; perfect English, modified with the slight softening burr you hear in a native Cumbrian. This was an educated man, and I couldn't help wondering at the circumstances that must have brought them together.

"His needs are few . . ." Dixter let the statement fade away. "He lives simply and humbly, and it is my pleasure to provide a space for his small home." Dixter watched my reactions, leaving a silent space of several moments before adding, "He is a remarkable teacher, as you will have observed."

Don Pedro leaned forward, huffed away such nonsense and broke the moment with: "Won't fit in caravan, if you carry on!" He took in a huge breath before beginning to push his bulk out of what I now saw was a full size, if not an oversized camping chair. The master now rose above his pupil, dwarfed, close to the ground. The sheer physical presence made me feel slightly intimidated.

In the next second, two things happened: Pedro leapt, in a golden flash, from his former seating position on Don Pedro's straightening knees and onto mine, pushing me past the balance point; and Don Pedro said softly, "Trust!" looking directly at me with more power than I have ever seen eyes hold.

The world stopped. The slow-motion space that contained it had an arc of movement that held a travelling pupil and a wise dog. Just before my head hit the hard tire rimmed with rusty metal, a soft hand came out of space, and Maria Angeles arrested my downward plunge, with the strong arm of a serving girl and a gentle kiss on the top of my head.

XIV

It was probably about time, I think.

Not 'about time' in the sense of being late for something important, no – literally about time.

There was a moment when the stars, shining on the tiny caravan's walls, got brighter. But, as this corresponded with a diminished ability to speak, created, undoubtedly, by the downing of the fourth or fifth glass of red wine, provided by my new friend, George Dixter, who can tell?

Don Pedro had gone – presumably to bed in his bijoux dwelling, but I hadn't seen it rock, and surely it would, with his weight entering it? Dixter was sitting next to me, sharing the last bottle of red. I think Maria Angeles was just behind my right shoulder, but I couldn't be sure.

Place and the importance of place seemed to be drifting away.

And then it happened:

I suddenly felt safer than I had ever done in my remembered life; as though normal, ordinary life contained a tension that I had got used to, a parasitic presence that masked the real taste of a freer life, where it simply dropped away in the face of a greater truth, one entirely at home with the sense of a light-filled trust present in every atom around and within us . . .

You may be forgiven for thinking that magic mushrooms had been in use, but I can assure you that was not the case. We had simply talked for hours, around a small but warm fire that Dixter had built in a grate against the stone wall.

"They'd think us crazy if we tried to talk about this . . ." It was Dixter speaking. His precise voice, with its soft but perfect rendering of English, was very soothing.

"I remember the first time I entered this state," he said,

leaning forward and filling my glass with the last of the Merlot. "I couldn't believe it was that simple!"

I managed to turn a head that was rapidly escaping the boundaries of motor control, and stared at him, quizzically.

"You mean it's always there?" I managed.

"Yes," he replied, pleased. "It's us who move away from it, not the other way around."

"But why?" I asked with difficulty over the 'w'.

"Why do we do it?" he replied.

"Yes."

"Because everyone in our lives lives with the tension of not-being, so we just do what humans do best, and copy . . ."

"So," I was beginning to slur, slightly. "How do we make its presence more repeat-able?" I had to drag out the last word into two syllables.

"Oh that's easy," he said.

"Hmm?"

"You just have to acknowledge that everything you've ever learned . . . is wrong."

He let that hang in the air, while he bent forward to push back a burning log that was threatening to escape the small grate.

"Is wrong . . ." I managed.

"Yusss" he said, the voice almost a whisper.

"All of it?" I managed.

"Well, enough of it . . . and all of it except what you need to do."

"Need to dooo?"

This was getting difficult – not the concepts, which were crystal clear; but the words.

I could sense that he knew he was losing me. He leaned towards me and formed his fingers into a pyramid shape under his nose.

"Doing is in the world. It's necessary, and why we're here. Seeing is what should precede Doing and is completely missing in modern life."

"Wrong . . . 'cos it's not this?" I managed, quite proud of the complex verbal construct I'd just put together.

"Exactly," he said. "We're not sitting in the driver's seat."

"'en, where are we?" I asked, whispering conspiratorially, in a way I suddenly found hugely amusing.

"That," he matched the whisper, "should you remember any of this in the morning, is your next task!" His glass chinked against mine, good naturedly, and we both drank deeply.

And then I drifted . . . and the stars got brighter still. And, suddenly, Maria Angeles emerged from behind my right shoulder and pulled me, firmly, to my feet, guiding me the short distance to the door of Don Pedro's caravan.

"Up you go," she said, the gentleness in her voice matching that of her actions.

I managed the small step, not questioning why I was being put in Don Pedro's home. Before me, what I had taken to be the twinkling light of the stars turned out to be the flames of seven coloured candles. The interior of Don Pedro's caravan was simple and truly beautiful. There was no-one else here. Maria Angeles pushed me towards the bed and the next to last thing I remember was her taking off my shoes and covering me up with a duvet.

"We all have a welcome," she said. "One day you will do it for another . . ."

Again, she kissed me on the head and left, closing the door with a: "Sleep well, I'll be back in the morning."

The very last thing I remember was the warmth of a snuggly Pomeranian lying across my feet on top of the duvet. It was a very welcome sensation. And then there was only the night and the trust and the stars . . .

XV

I awoke, slowly, and began a routine of what I used to think of as self-recovery – a technique not used for many years, since my wilder youth . . .Not to move – that was the key! Take a complete snapshot of the situation, including mental state and any 'must remember' thoughts from the dark womb of sleep just departed, before even raising a finger . . .

I remembered where I was. I also remembered how much red wine I had drunk. I opened one eye and looked around me. The curtains of the tiny caravan were closed and a gentle light filtered through. A small window was open and a breeze played softly through the curtains and into the interior. So far so good.

I risked a further movement. The slight turn of my head revealed a small table next to the bed. On the table were an old glass jug and a matching glass. Both contained water. The jug was nearly empty; the glass still half full, as though containing the remainder of a life-saving hydration. Could I have been that clever, back then in the flickering night? I sat up. Nothing, no pounding head or wrenching guts. Still suspicious, I eased myself off the bed and set my feet on the floor, expecting the room to begin spinning. Again, nothing.

I looked around. There was a small towel draped over the tiny sink. Gingerly, I got to my feet and rested my palms on the sink's stainless steel edges. Taking off my creased shirt, I pumped the single tap to get some cold water into the sink and began to wash myself. The shock of the icy water shredded the last vestiges of sleep. Ten minutes later, I stepped down from the caravan and onto the site of our impromptu picnic.

The little garden had been tidied. There were no signs of last night's party. The camping chairs had been flattened and stashed under a canvas, along with the folding table. In the distance was the sound of someone whistling. I threw my jacket over my shoulder and followed the noise. It was hideously out of tune, but had a great deal of energy and enthusiasm. I think it was a 60s pop song, being murdered, horribly, but, so bad was the carnage, it was hard to be sure.

George Dixter was standing, knee deep in hay, in the middle of a large barn. For once, he wasn't wearing his long khaki raincoat. Dressed in a checked shirt, with old brown cord trousers and wellingtons, he was forking the hay from the residue of a smaller pile to the growing heap of another. The interior of the barn was partly given over to use as a stable, and three horses were ambling around in the far corner. Looking very contented as they fed. Dixter saw me and looked up, smiling. I began to walk towards him, but he 'pushed' me back with his hand. It was a powerful gesture and I felt that he had practically made contact with my midsection. I stopped and looked at him. His smile continued and he waved in an unmistakable gesture that indicated it was time for me to leave.

His action brought on a powerful emotion of rejection. Had I offended them? Not wishing to abuse, further, by my continued presence, I tried my best to hide the emotion. I waved my thanks and turned to go. After all, I needed to get home and shower. Thus rationalised, I began the walk into town. As I ambled along, the air began to refresh me, and, by the time I reached Grange, I was hungry. I decided I would visit the café for some coffee and toast before I collected the car, which I hoped would still be unclamped in the nearby car park.

I sat in our usual table. I had half hoped to see Maria Angeles, but another woman served me – a fiery redhead, tall and quite severe looking, somewhat older than Maria Angeles, but still with a youthfulness about her. She was just what I didn't need, I thought to myself as she dropped my coffee and toast onto the table top, nearly spilling them.

My internal state was very confused. I felt as though I had done something wrong – and yet, when I thought back to the blissful and warm evening before, I could find nothing. I had joined in their party – and found out that it had also belonged to me. So why was I now so insecure? I tried stepping back from my state, in the way that Don Pedro had indicated. I could feel how far I was from my 'centre'. My heart was racing with anxiety; my breathing was unsteady; there was even a tension in my gut. What a mess! In truth, I felt the very opposite to the way I had been the night before. Was this all fabricated on their part? Were they showing me these contrasts deliberately, showing me how fragile these ego states were?

With that thought, the redhead brought the bill, which she dropped onto the table next to me. I looked down at the chipped saucer. It held what looked like an envelope. This was a bit elaborate for a simple bill! Feeling quite queasy, I examined it, suspiciously. It was fastened with a wax seal across the join on the rear. The seal bore no relation to anything I had ever seen. I turned the envelope over.

Written across the front were the words: 'To the wolf with no name'.

I coughed, partly suppressing the shocked warble that

came from the back of my throat. Feeling acutely self-conscious, I looked back at the café, not wanting the redhead to be a witness to my chagrin. She was standing by the door, clearing another of the tables, but she was looking at me. As our eyes made contact, I sensed that she had not tried to hide it – that it was all part of some elaborate mind-game, the smirk she displayed as she carried her tray into the café's interior said it all. But perhaps it was just a smile, interpreted, angrily, by a man whose smooth veneer had just cracked.

Unwilling to share the last part of this drama, I stood and jammed the envelope into my jacket pocket. I dropped some coins into the saucer – enough to pay for the unopened bill, and left. The car was mercifully unclamped, but the warden was hovering. I started the engine, spun the gravel rather childishly, and drove away.

XVI

But, the anger didn't get me far . . . The past few months had begun to change me. I could no longer react to a situation and stay, blind, to that response. Somewhere in the country lanes between Grange and Cark, I had to stop at a rail crossing where I sat with the anger – not trying to change it, simply being present to it. As I did so, I could feel which part of 'me' was feeling it . . . and it wasn't anything authentic; it wasn't where I had chosen to live. It prickled as I distanced myself from it, watching its actions. In that moment, a new space inside me had its birth. The sheer emotion of the moment, the sense of uncertainty, the presence of an opening in time, space and life before me, all conspired to change my reality.

Had they known this would be the response? Could they really have plotted this, or did their plan have just a vague outline, a space for possibilities, a canvas on which some other agency would paint the minute detail, the usually-missed symphony of life unfolding, experienced as a taken-for-granted stew . . .

And then, a different feeling emerged – there in the incongruity of a level crossing, with an old, but still visible diesel spill darkening the broken tarmac beneath the car, like an old map. I got out to look at the approaching train. I knew that they wouldn't work to that level of manipulative detail, because the journey didn't belong to them – it belonged to me . . . I breathed in the clear air of that thought as the train hurtled past me, a few feet from my face. The metaphor was perfect, a hurtling train, with passengers constrained, like humanity, to travel together.

They – we – travelled in certain patterns of normality, through time. The only way to break that was to get off the train. And there I was, standing to one side of it, at least for the moment, in a way that belonged, uniquely, to my own life.

The sheer intensity of that moment – which seemed to challenge everything that I had been before in my life, brought on a profound sense of quiet. I returned to the car and sat, quietly, waiting for the gates to rise and listening to the power of that silence. The crossing's gates were still down, indicating that another train was due.

I had a strong sense of not wishing to recover; of letting this be one of a thousand deaths of the old me; wondering if this was the ferryman's price for passage to that new land. Something with extreme vitality flowed and danced before my eyes, invisible to all but the quietest of the senses.

I had opened the driver's window and found I was looking down at the diesel stain on the road. In the shifting light of the early autumn day, it reminded me of a drawing of Humphrey Head. Even the relief contours of the long hill were briefly sketched by the morning sun refracting through a nearby tree. Then a cloud passed over the sun and the illusion was lost. A goods train thundered through the small junction, taking a while for its endless trucks to pass through the crossing. Eventually, the crossing barrier clanked upwards and I was free to continue the journey.

I had taken a long way home, to provide me with time to think. My meandering route had taken me near to the place so recently sketched out on the stained road. I smiled and thought about that – I was free to interpret the moment as I chose – but I was getting used to the idea that one should leave open an array of possibilities at each such juncture. There were many benefits to this way of thinking. One was that it tended to negate the habitual inner voice of 'what's going to happen next'. Not having the faintest idea of what was going to happen next was a powerful ally in the process of staying in this truly magical state of mind.

Humphrey Head. . . . I thought about the 'map of light and shadow' that had appeared on the roadway. The ancient and high land mass that jutted out into the northern coast of Morecambe bay had been the site of the first glimpse into the oddity of their world – that picnic on the grass, finding which had produced an amazing feeling of what I had only been able to describe as homecoming.

I wondered if I dared consider that there could be, again, something waiting for me on the Head. I stopped the car and took the unopened envelope out of my jacket pocket. I studied the glyph on the back of it.

The main part of the design was definitely a letter 'W'. The dot was large and didn't appear to belong to the letter below. Putting aside consideration of the dot, I concentrated on the letter. "W' could stand for many things, but I had an idea that their earlier references to my nickname of 'Lobo' was related to this. I had never been called a wolf before – but it seemed to be part of their teaching system to assign such a name. I wondered if they also knew that Humphrey Head is, according to local legend, reputed to be the place where the last wolf in England was shot. Whether or not they knew that, I reasoned that the "W" had to refer to me. The dot would explain itself in time . . .

I tore the envelope open. Inside was a single, folded sheet of plain paper. In very neat hand-writing was written:

"One word underlies all others . . . find it"

I stared at the paper. 'finding it' could be so many things. I had the sense that it was not an intellectual reference. It was more likely to be geographic. If that were the case, then Humphrey Head was worth another visit. It took me only fifteen more minutes to get to the car park by the tidal shoreline. The tide was far out so I felt safe parking there, on the edge of the shifting sands of Morecambe Bay.

I locked the car, wondering what I was doing. One half of my mind resented being there. It wanted to be home and bathing, it couldn't understand what sort of fool's errand its errant twin was undertaking. A few minutes later, I rounded the corner that led to the start of the footpath . . . and stopped, staring at the base of a large stone that marked the way. On it, in two colours of chalk, was drawn an image, a negative of the one on my envelope:

XVII

Perhaps I had expected a winding trail of clues, leading up Humphrey Head, to a hidden nook, where I would find them all giggling at me? But that would be too trite – and that wasn't their style.

Perhaps Maria Angeles, mysteriously missing from most of the previous evening's festivities, would be there, alone, to escort me, romantically, across the lovely landscape of the Head, accompanied by a barking Pedro.

What I hadn't expected was to find Don Pedro himself, sitting, alone, on an old bench, just beyond the entrance stone on which they had chalked the mysterious 'W' symbol.

He greeted me with a warm smile and a handshake. Both were somewhat unnerving.

"Big journey," he nodded his head in approval. "But you get here?" he asked, in the broken English that I suspected was part of his trademark persona.

I looked at his corpulent face, noting the absence of his usual, irascible expression – which I knew to be entirely manufactured. Today, he seemed to be in a quieter mood. He stood up and indicated we should walk up the path.

"Lobo does well, this far," he said, using my Wolf nickname and picking up the pace as we began to climb in earnest. I was always surprised at how fit he was, for such a big man. "Now we see how well he think . . ."

Another few minutes saw us cresting the first ridge, the level at which the sheep seemed to reside. I thought back to that first trip in the early summer, when I had raced up the hill to find he and Maria Angles picnicking in a hidden hollow – an almost surreal experience. The sheep had seemed significant on that day.

Sheep had always been an important symbol for me. I had nothing against the actual animals, but the idea of people as 'sheep' bothered me greatly. I had always considered that so much of humanity's time was spent not thinking about important things, and wasting life on the trivial. The idea of people blindly following each other in the movement of the herd had always been a trigger for my actions to the reverse – reactionary, my mother had called it. She had been right – I had carried this too far, of course. My youth had seen me ostracised by many other pupils at school because I was judgemental and too 'stand-offish'. How good life is at rounding off those rough edges . . .

Don Pedro smiled, as though reading my expression.

"But you softer, now . . ."

He had picked up so well on that nuance – 'softer'. Not as in being soft, just gentler with myself and the world, too. Did he miss nothing?

"Acceptance is hard lesson," he picking up the pace again. I was actually getting breathless trying to keep up with him "But unless we accept, there no reality!"

I thought about this. "Why not, Don Pedro," I asked.

"When we resist what is before eyes," he pointed two fingers are himself as though he was about to stab his own. "We introduce the slayer."

"The slayer?"

"Yes, he kill present, the slayer."

I walked in silence for a while, musing on this. He had positioned the 'slayer' as a thing antagonistic to the present, a killer of some precious quality in the now. His slayer was therefore something from the past. I walked on, thinking deeply. Moments later, I realised that I could no longer hear his footfalls. I turned to look for him. He was about a hundred metres behind me and drawing something in an exposed piece of ground, using a stick.

"You figured out slayer?" he asked, his face a huge grin.

"Not yet," I replied. "But I'm working on it."

"Good," he said. "Then we add this, too . . ."

I looked down to see that he had drawn a strange shape in the dirt.

"What is it, Don Pedro."

"It map of human love, life and light," he said. "It map of struggle, help and goal. There nothing of importance that it not."

I reproduce it here, from my notebook, done a few hours later, after I had, finally showered, and fallen into bed. It remains a pivotal moment in my life, rendered, from a sense of urgency, just before I fell asleep, again.

XVIII - XXIX
The Beast at the Door

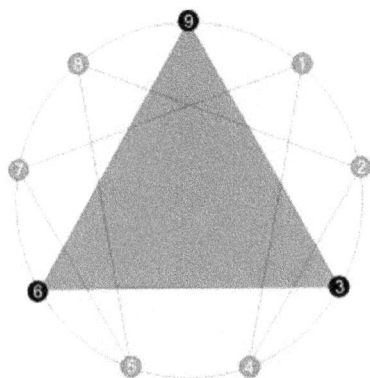

XVIII

I had seen the geometric figure before, but didn't know what it was. I stared at it, drawn crudely in the earth, and asked him what it meant.

"It called Enneagram," he said softly, as though embracing something precious with the words.

"It how we teach."

"What do you teach, Don Pedro?" I asked.

"Teach forgetting," he responded immediately, as though reciting a powerful mantra.

With that, he used his foot to scrub out the interior of the drawn figure, leaving only the circle remaining. The action had separated, with rough textures, the exterior from the space within, which now looked chaotic.

"Chaotic . . ." I voiced the word, though I hadn't meant to. He gave me a sly look and smiled.

"Hold thought," he chuckled. "And recover shape inside."

I thought about word 'recover'. He had used it in a very precise way. I tried hard to remember how the figure had looked. I had counted nine points, before he rubbed it out, but I knew it hadn't all been regular. To start with, there had been a triangle in there, and something else.

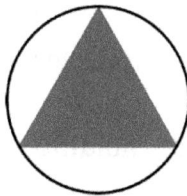

He watched me wrestle with the memory before walking on, higher up the Head. I followed him, recovering the strange geometric figure in my mind, beginning with the triangle I remembered. I have a decent memory and find that using colours to emphasise shape can help with remembering. Since we were surrounded by the green of Humphrey Head, I used it, mentally, to create my image.

Near the top of the head there is a plateau which extends along the western edge of the landmass for about fifty metres. In the middle of this he knelt and picked up part of a large fallen branch. He stood, again, and used it to draw out a much larger circle in the earth, enclosing a clump of wild grasses within. Looking at me to check I was present to what he was doing, he then used the heel of his large boot to drag a zigzag line round the perimeter, rendering the ground immediately on the outside of the circle into the same churned soil that had been within the former, smaller one.

I watched, fascinated. Soon, he had finished and was standing within the circle. He looked at me, with a huge grin filling his corpulent face.

"See difference?" he asked.

"Between the circles?" I responded.

"Part, but bigger difference," he began to rock with laughter. I looked at the large circle he had drawn and his mirthful figure within it.

"Well," I added, trying to recover some authority. "The first circle had a rough – chaotic – interior, whereas this one has a chaotic exterior." I felt quite proud of this summary, though its content was fairly obvious. However, the mocking grin lingered on his face.

"More?" he asked, holding the implacable wall of challenge.

I felt a certain degree of ire rise up in me. There was, clearly, an important lesson here, and I had the feeling that it was, literally, staring me in the face. I looked at his large figure and realised he was standing in the exact centre of the drawn circle. With relief, I blurted it out.

"Of course – you're in the centre of the circle!"

"And you?"

"I'm not," I said, trying to break the tension." He nodded, good naturedly, but his face said there was more to come.

"You like to be centre of circle?' He asked, with a hint of mock conspiracy; at the same time opening his huge arms in a gesture that could not be mistaken.

I moved to join him, but he stopped me as I was about to cross the perimeter of the circle.

"Not there!" he said. It was more of a command than a statement, though there was gentleness in it.

I looked up to see he was pointing to another place on the circle's rim.

"Where the sun, rises," he said. "East . . ."

I moved around the circumference until I was level with his finger. Watching him nod as I approached it. I felt the need to take a breath as I began to cross over the threshold, but he barked out another command, "Mark it!"

I froze. Then, catching on to his meaning, I ground my heel into the dirt, making a mark that defined this, the Eastern point on the circle.

"Good. Now three paces around to here." His pointing arm and extended figure made a second virtual intersection with the circumference. He watched as I did my best to pace the three steps equally. He had obviously marked out the circle to accommodate my stride, and I had to marvel at his skill in this.

No sooner had I marked the second spot when he repeated the instruction, pointing to a third point that would complete the three. Now familiar with what he wanted, I completed the 'heel points' and he directed me back to the start, the point he had called East.

"Now, join me," he said, with a very different tone that was almost parental.

Soon, I was standing in the centre of a circle we had both drawn. No sooner had I arrived at the centre, than he began to spin me around, facing first the East, then rotating me to face the second point I had marked, which was clearly neither West nor South, since it lay one third the way around the circle. Without giving me time for further consideration, he spun me around to face the next point – one equally out of phase with the cardinal directions, but an intrinsic part of the whole. Completing the circle with my spinning figure, he let me pause for a second facing East, then used his huge strength to spin me in complete circles faster, gaining momentum with each second.

I found this invasion of my body-space very disturbing. Here I was, ostensibly on my way home, unwashed, being spun around by a man I had reluctantly accepted as my teacher. As my body spun faster and faster, I felt something snap within me. As though he had sensed this release of resistance, Don Pedro brought my rotation to a gentle standstill.

Dizzy, I faced the East, though the world was now whirling in a sensation that reminded me of childhood games.

"Stay a while and think on where you are . . " he said, gently, giving my shoulders a final squeeze before walking from the centre to the East, then turning and placing a hand over his heart before leaving.

My head still spinning, I stood and listened to his fading footfalls. Soon, I was alone in the middle of a spinning circle on the top of the Head.

XIX

The autumnal winds were blowing straight off the shore and across the front of the Sunrise Tearooms. The summer had definitely gone. I tightened the collar of my jacket around my scarf to preserve my body warmth. I had not seen any of them for two weeks. I had stayed away from Grange, wanting to review what had happened to me – what kept happening to me.

They were an unusual group. I had never encountered anything like this, before, and I viewed myself as a reasonably well-read student of the spiritual. It was as though their goal was to cut through much of the mystical teaching of the past, and present the results as a very direct – and often abrupt – method of approaching the target.

But what was their target?

The act of 'stopping the world' was what had first awakened my real attention. I knew the technique had not originated with their group. I had read of similar things from books published decades ago. The idea was simple – to create an internal tension with an unusual action, such that the normal 'flow' of the world around was interrupted. When this happened, there was a sense of something breaking.

I sipped my coffee – it was nearly cold, its weak heat doing little, now, to offset my loss of warmth, sitting obstinately on the terrace of the café, with a couple of people smoking as my only company. I must have looked strange – ridiculous, even . . . Yet, something stubborn in me clung to this action. It was, after all, how Don Pedro and I had met. This, too, was an act of stopping the world, a breaking of the normal, the expected.

What was it that broke under such circumstances?

They had made no attempt to contact me since the strange but wonderful ritual on the Head. I felt as though this period of reflection was normal, was expected. Then I caught myself in this thought and realised my mind was avoiding answering the question I had just posed by injecting a vivid memory into my consciousness.

What was it that broke under such circumstances?

Could my mind be taking me away from answering that very question? And why would it? Why would my greatest ally – my ability to think – be trying to derail an inner question whose importance had already been set by my will? I brought my focus back to the question, again: how could the act of doing something deliberately different, and in some cases, quite antisocial, generate that sense of tearing? I held the question this time, would not let any other thought displace it. Within a few seconds the inner dialogue ceased, the sense of wrestling with it calmed; and I found myself staring at something deep within me.

When stopping the world worked, it was because a deeper part of me came to life. Smiling, it emerged from the place it always lived and gained access to the 'normal' world in a different way. Across from me, a woman in a fur coat took out an elegant lighter to finish her coffee with a cigarette which already sat in her painted, red lips. I had spent several seconds fascinated by the tableau, when I realised that I had done it again – my attention had been consumed by the 'world' just as I was getting somewhere.

How strong was this force?

For some reason, the circle that Don Pedro had traced on Humphrey Head came to mind. Was that shape related to this new sense of 'me'? Perhaps 'me' was the wrong word for it, since 'me' described my normal sense of self, and this newly-revealed inner being was quite different. Why had I never seen into myself before in this way?

Before I could probe this further, a hand that actually felt warm, through the layers of my jacket, fell on my shoulder and a light kiss was planted on my head.

"Lobo deep in thought," said a familiar soft and teasing voice. "Fresh coffee?"

I turned my head to smile up at her. Although dressed in her work uniform, she looked beautiful.

"It's cold out here." Her head inclined slightly and the brown eyes blazed a kind of inner fire.

"Shall I put the coffee on one of the nice warm tables inside?"

I watched her measure my response with eyes that didn't even flicker. I had the sense that I could revisit this moment a hundred times and fail. I needed to continue acting in a way that would avoid any of my usual comforts, to keep that link to what I had just found alive.

I smiled back at her and shook my head, almost imperceptibly. I swear that I actually felt a flash of energy pass from those brown orbs. She nodded her head, without words, and turned to bring my coffee out to my cold world . . .

But my inner world was blazing . . .

XX

What was it that broke under such circumstances?

I had asked the question of myself the week before. When you 'stopped the world' what was it that broke? Perhaps breaking was too strong a word – it could also be described as a passage from one state of attention to another . . . I sipped the hot coffee, noisily – it was the only way to drink it, fresh from the flask.

"Penny for them?" asked George Dixter, sitting on the park bench next to me. We had bumped into each other the day before, and he had offered croissants and coffee in the park; the place where I had first met him. The weather had turned damp and cold, so he didn't look out of place in his old Burberry mac, which seemed to accompany him everywhere and in all seasons. On this occasion, and, no doubt in deference to the late autumn, he was also wearing an olive green fedora.

In the late fifties or even sixties, he would have cut quite a contemporary dash. But now, he looked like a character out of a period spy movie. I smiled at the thought, but was wary – little that these people did appeared to be accidental.

"Well, two things . . ." I sipped some more of his generously provided coffee and gratefully accepted the fresh croissant which had been procured from the bakery across the road from the park.

"Firstly," my grin widened as his snakey eyes locked onto mine. Conspiratorially, I lowered my voice. "Why the George Smiley outfit?"

He leaned closer, playing the perfect spy, and whispered, ". . . And secondly?"

I couldn't help it, I chuckled. "Well, secondly, what is it that breaks when we 'stop the world'.

"Aha . . ." he said, sitting back and mirroring my noisy sipping of the ultra-hot coffee, as though he had just learned some secret from me.

"Well now," he began, putting down his steaming coffee and flexing his fingers outwards from linked palms. "the first one is easier to answer – play!"

"Play?" I asked, unsure if it were noun or command.

"Yes, play," he replied. "as in we don't play enough!"

"We?"

"We, as in people," he replied good-naturedly. "We forget how to play and play is really important!"

I thought about this for a while, while he sipped his coffee. I was about to ask another question when he answered it. "My outfit, as you say, is quirky . . . It makes me feel good because, in it, I'm playing; and I love the reaction of those around me, and it would help stop their worlds if they used it properly – which brings us, nicely, to your second question . . ."

I considered the import of what he had said. They were all playing . . . and yet.

"What breaks," he continued, leaning closer, again and emphasising the serious side of this play. "is something that hides behind the habitual, which we call the slayer of the now."

They had mentioned the word slayer, before. I knew it meant something in Buddhism, but I was not sure if they used it in the same way.

"So, stopping the world is an example of an action that defeats the slayer?"

"Yes, as, to a certain extent, does the whole idea of play." He sipped the last of his coffee and looked at his watch. "Play and stopping the world makes us present to the moment, the now. The real lives only in the now, the rest is a system of mental devices which support the slayer . . ."

He looked at his watch. "I must go." He said, holding out

his hand for my coffee cup which was part of a set belonging to the large flask. It was still half full, but I handed it back to him, expecting that he would empty it onto the nearby grass. He didn't – instead he reached into his canvas shoulder bag and pulled out a Styrofoam cup. Emptying the remainder into this, he passed it back to me.

"You'll be delighted to learn that Maria Angelo has offered to take the next bit with you!"

Events were happening too fast. I blurted out, "When?"

"It's on the bottom of the cup," he replied, striding off around the path.

Carefully, I raised the foam cup and examined its underside. There was nothing. I moved to protest at the departing back of the raincoat, but he beat me to it.

"Oh yes it is . . ." he shouted over his shoulder.

I stared at the cup more carefully. On its rim, three marks had been added with a blue Biro. They formed a perfect triangle within the circle. I chuckled, again, thinking of my last meeting up there with Don Pedro. So, it was to be on Humphrey Head, again, but when?

Five minutes later, when my musings on the meeting were finished, I downed the last of the coffee, only to find emerging from the dregs at the bottom of the cup the words 'Thursday next, 3.00 p.m.'

XXI

The wind howled through the thin branches of the tree, bent at nearly ninety degrees to the vertical by a lifetime of unremitting force. I could imagine that only on the best days of summer would there be quiet up there, on the highest point of Humphrey Head.

Maria Angeles watched me study the tree around which she had just walked, wordlessly, three times. She had not spoken on the whole ascent; meeting me, in silence, at the small car park below with a wordless smile and little else. I had dutifully followed her up and across what had been green sheep meadows when I had been here in the spring – back at the start of all this; but the sheep were gone. This day contained only the pale grass of December and the biting wind.

She watched me as I considered the tree. I was learning to let the moment take me; to allow the mind to be still long enough for that which lies beneath thought to emerge – and act. And its actions now revealed so much about this special place they used. The high point was no accident – I knew that the 'hill' has long been a generic for that which takes you away from 'the world'; although the use of 'world' in this context is misleading, as there is, most certainly a real world out there, which has as much to teach us as the inner . . .

And that was the rub . . . the real world was not a thing, it was a totality . . . and I was beginning to see the vast difference between the two. In the whole you can find the true part, but in the part you can never find the whole. Only by beginning with wholes can we have our eyes opened. Finding the whole required different thinking, or, ideally, no thinking at all . . .

Maria Angeles watched me intently, still silent. She stood with great composure, as though measuring my thoughts and outside of time, but not outside of event.

After a few seconds, her eyes flickered with something and a gentle smile played across her lips. She took my hand and placed me with my back against the lone tree, so that its wind-blown extension was behind me and facing away – following the direction of the prevailing wind. Still smiling, she placed a finger over my lips. I understood the unspoken instruction and said nothing, letting the moment, and the wind, flow around me.

Moving backwards, she held my eyes like a snake. She stopped when she reached the edge of the unmarked circle around which she had carried out the three circuits. I looked intensely at her, trying to read the bright energy in her unblinking eyes. As though pulling that mental and emotional contact with her, she turned her head to the left, but let her eyes move more slowly, in an action that reminded me of Egyptian wall paintings . . . I suddenly realised that the gesture had 'stopped the world' for both of us. . .

Don't move – but follow . . . said the eyes. Follow.

She began a slow circuit, and I felt I was watching it through those eyes – not literally, but emotionally. From the point at which her full gaze had been on me, I could feel the changing characteristics of our relative positions. Now, she had reached the first quadrant, at ninety degrees to my right. Like a man watching the setting sun, I was losing her immediate, visual presence. Another quadrant, and I could feel her directly behind, me. There came a sensation of what I can only describe as something boring into my back, just behind the neck, and then it flashed through me as a kind of heat in my symbolic isolation.

She was moving again, and beginning to appear in my left vision, where she stopped and smiled. I knew she was smiling, even though I couldn't see it. Finally, she began the last quarter circle, returning to gaze, fully, at me, from her start point.

Both her hands beckoned. The tenderness with which she

held them out was palpable. Come, said the gesture, come.

I walked the radius to stand with her, taking her hands. In the biting wind, they were warm. Life, said a voice in my head, life.

She spun me round, to look back at the lone tree. I was now standing with my back to the wind, looking at the bent bush as though I were part of the force that had created its deformity. My mind began to feel unreal. I was part of something much bigger than its feeble and petty interests. I was part of Life . . .

She pushed me gently, back towards the tree, again. I leaned forward to move with her unspoken instructions; but, immediately, she pulled me back to her, as though showing that she would not let me return to that place, unchanged, no matter what the natural and habitual forces of attraction . . . As our bodies were reunited, I could feel her warmth, even through the layers of winter clothing we both wore.

And then she spun me to the left and guided me around the first quadrant of the imaginary circle. Turning me, there, to look at the lone tree, again. I felt I was seeing it with eyes very different to before. There it stood, alive but bent, at an angle to the world that had been determined long before its birth. I wanted to shout out, I felt irrational anger – I wanted to defend it. It had no choices, I cried, voicelessly, to the wind.

Sensing this, Maria Angeles gripped me tightly; and spun me around in a tight circle, coming back to face the lone tree, again. Empowered? I thought . . . but there was no time to consider it further. I was marched on and spun to face the lone tree from the downwind side. What did this mean? The other side, the windward side, clearly represented the natural forces of life; but here? I was at the position to which the tree was seemingly being pulled. And yet there was no pulling force, just the push of the eternal wind . . . Illusion, my silent voice, said softly. See it for what it is . . . There is only one force . . .

Once more, there was no time to think, and soon I was facing the tree across the circle from the point where the empathetic anger had gripped me. Here, there arose a feeling for which I had no definite words – a mixture of wanting to act combined with a sense of realism. My movements in Maria Angelo's circle had a freedom that the tree had not; and yet the tree was our focus. We brought possibility to this world, where the tree, alone, had little, if any . . .

And then we were back to the windward point, and she turned me to face the tree again. This time, I hesitated, and could feel her smile, even though I could not see her face. She waited . . . and waited. There was something required of me at this place, some gesture that would demonstrate that my new knowledge had at least begun to be transformed into understanding.

Seized with initiative, I turned slowly, clockwise to face her.

Her smile was radiant. She reached out gentle arms and embraced me. Then, she pulled away, but not before giving me a flashing look that said we would visit this spot many times . . .

When her wordless and dancing figure had fallen below the line of visibility from the summit, I backed towards the bent lone tree and let the feeling of its presence seep into me. It was a beautiful thing, full of strength and capable of standing up to the winds that razed this peak. But, it had no choices in the world, and had been bent by a lifetime of force.

But I did have choices . . .

Something bright in front of me took my attention. I looked back along the line to the windward point – the last place that Maria Angelo had occupied before she left the circle, our circle. On the ground was a white envelope. I walked towards it and bent to pick it up. On the front was written my name – my circle name, came the flash: Lobo. I thought about this Spanish reference to 'wolf'. It was an image wild and full of potential, and

I had liked it the first time they had used it for me. Wolf . . . Lobo. I let the word run through my mind as I opened the envelope.

Inside, and responsible for the weight that had prevented it blowing away in the strong December wind, were a card and three coins. I looked at the card and smiled . . .

XXII

Where was all this going? I wondered, as I walked along the Grange seafront on a dismal day. So many wonderful things had happened, so why was I feeling such a sense of unease? To go from the 'high' on Humphrey Head, in the gentle care of Maria Angelo, to a slump like this was not characteristic of me. I am normally an optimistic person, so I needed to get to the bottom of this feeling.

I knew myself well enough to know that I can also be quite lazy with such things. To counter this, and to bring myself into the 'now' with some force, I decided to forgo my usual coffee at the Sunrise tearooms and walk along the shore – gloomy or not – until I had some resolution of this negative emotion.

And so I walked and talked to myself, sorting my thoughts into a sequence of ideas.

1. I knew I'd been lucky – very lucky – to meet such a spiritual group of people in a place like Grange-over-Sands.

2. They were dynamic and quite formidable. I wanted, as the saying goes, to continue to be 'in their company'.

3. I had been quite open with my feelings, allowing them to carry out their 'alchemy' to shift my longstanding views of the world.

4. This process had worked well.

5. So why the hell was I feeling so low!

I sat on a bench and determined to do an 'enquiry' on myself. I had read about this technique many years ago. Its popular use seemed to come out of the Human Potential Movement in California in the 1960s. It is a very simple thing, and comprises holding in your mind something that is troubling you or which you wish to consider in more depth. The essence of it is to ask it questions, then let the answers take you . . .

following their thread without judgment, and with an open inner 'eye'.

I knew what my opening question should be: "What am I feeling?"

I watched my mind actually recoil from the question! There was a pause as I let the calmness settle in, then I asked it again, and watched as a kind of inner distance emerged between 'me' and the state of mind I wanted to understand. The answer came back with a shock: "Fear".

I nearly lost the thread at that point, but just managed to hold on to my composure. I steadied my breathing, and took myself back to being present with the thread. I hadn't expected that answer. "Fear of what?" I asked my mind. It took a few moments for the threads of meaning to unravel, almost as if they were trying to escape.

The answer formed slowly: 'Diminishing".

At that point my inner dialogue was interrupted by a cry from my right.

Grange is a place of many sights. One of the most unusual is a behemoth of a footbridge that crosses the Lancaster – Barrow main line, half a mile to the west of Grange station. This tall, black structure would not have been out of place in the original film of H. G. Wells' War of the Worlds. It bestrides the tracks like a colossus, linking the west of the town with the seashore. The long climb up the forbidding gradient is quite steep, and from the other direction, young and old alike are often to be found picking their way, slowly, down it, to get to the seafront.

A young woman was screaming on the top of the footbridge, at the highest point of the slope. She pointed to her pram, which had begun to career out of control and was gathering speed as it bounced off the black rails. I leapt to my feet and crossed the short distance to the start of the slope, before dragging air into my lungs to prepare to sprint and intercept the runaway child's carrier. I met the buggy halfway down the slope, but only managed to take hold of its right side; with the result that, although I halted its momentum, it spun out of my grasp and fell onto its side, taking me down with it. Somewhat dazed, I dragged myself off the wet surface and clambered on my knees to peer into the interior of the buggy, hoping against hope that the infant had been strapped in.

The pram was empty. My heart was still thumping and I looked up to see the child's mother running down with her little boy in her arms. Her thanks were plentiful as she took my arm with her free one and helped me to my feet.

But she couldn't understand the look of shock and bemusement on my face.

I left, quickly, assuring her that I was fine, if a little scuffed . . . As I got to the top of the footbridge, I looked back to see her putting her son, securely, back into the buggy and adjusting his harness.

The picture of Don Pedro came into my mind. His image formed a layer over my thoughts – seemingly urging me to see this incident as something significant. Five minutes later, and still shaking, I entered the deserted terrace of the Sunrise café. The interior looked warm and inviting. Surely I could permit myself some change to the rigours of our outdoor teaching place on such an occasion?

As I opened the outer door, a golden fox looked up at me with sad eyes. Pedro refused to budge as I said my hellos to him and stroked his warm head.

A few seconds later, the inner door opened and there stood Maria Angelo with a steaming mug of coffee. She took my arm with her free hand and directed us both to sit in the cold and windy terrace.

She seemed to know I had been through an experience

that had shaken me up, but said nothing while my equilibrium returned. These people wasted nothing, and seemed to see significance written in everything.

But the coffee was warm and the company was wonderful.

XXIII

We had made no plans to meet up on this first day of the new year. I had received no invitations. So why was I driving to Grange-over-Sands to park the car as though this were one of our regular gatherings?

I knew the Sunrise Café would be closed. It was freezing cold, and a nasty south-westerly had come in overnight and was doing its best to render the coast uninhabitable.

But drive I did – and felt a glowing sense of what I can only describe as involvement as I covered the fifteen miles along roads that were mainly empty. From a rational point of view, there was very little chance that they would be there. The silent café would hold no expectation of a warm Maria Angelo, standing there with my mug of steaming coffee. Still, I drove, putting aside the world of rational thought, willing myself to enter that different state of mind in which there is found the unexpected, the truly magical ...

I must have been the only one in the main street of the town as I gathered my long loden coat around me and fastened up its high neck, wrapped tightly around a woollen scarf. It had been a present to myself many years ago while on a business trip in The Hague, and so far had survived several of my annual garment culls. There was something wonderful about the way its tightly woven Tyrolean wool wrapped you from chin to shin; as if to say, in its cloth-like way, there, see, we can cope with anything now. In many ways it was a bit like a cloak, and I smiled at the unintended magical association as I strode, with great purpose and little expectation, up the steep street and past the long line of closed shops. I hadn't seen anyone wearing such a garment for years, but that rather enhanced how I felt on this new year's morning.

The Sunrise Café was closed, of course. Even the tables had been stacked to one side; and a hand-written note in the window explained that the family were on holiday, and the place would be shut until the end of January. I stood quietly and surveyed the space in which so much had happened in the past year. It had been a futile expectation that they would be there – they were probably huddled in Don Pedro's tiny caravan, filling it with warmth and cheer. I took one last look around the stacked tables, feeling sad that their weatherbeaten wooden surfaces could not contain my customary mug of coffee. I was about to leave when my eye was taken by a flash of tartan. I walked towards the far table, nearest the café's doorway, to examine what I had glimpsed.

An old-style thermos flask stood upright and propped out of the wind's fury. A piece of white paper had been rolled tightly and jammed into the handle of the outermost cup. Smiling in disbelief, I extracted it and read the note, which was in Don Pedro's untidy handwriting. It read: 'There is colder café down by shore – that one closed, too!'

It was a reference to our first meeting now so long ago ... and an unmistakable invitation.

Grinning like a child, I scooped the old tartan-patterned object into my gloved hands and ran. The path down to the promenade took me over the giant black walkway that had so recently been the scene of a very scary incident. But, throwing caution to the wind, which was now full into my face, I continued to run down its steep gradient, emerging breathless, onto the deserted prom.

Deserted, that is, apart from a group of figures hugging themselves in the empty garden of the Shore Café. A fourth member of their group, a fox-like object, was the first to see me, and ran to greet me as I rounded the end of the descending walkway. Pedro the Pomeranian was so enthused at our meeting, that I had to stop my forward movement to embrace his golden swirling, keeping careful hold of the full flask in my left hand.

Eventually, he turned his head to look for his master, Don Pedro.

When I finally looked up, they were smiling. I approached with a huge grin on my face, clutching the flask like an entry ticket. There were hugs, but nothing was said. They had congregated around a wooden garden table, constructed in a triangular design. Don Pedro waved me to consider the picnic laid out in pieces of greaseproof paper. Essentially, it was a small feast of Christmas leftovers. Mince pies, past their best, but still serviceable, vied with assorted pieces of cheese and some fresh French bread. There was an assortment of festive biscuits to finish the meal.

"Need bigger table for next year!" Don Pedro grinned, breaking the silence and waving me towards the food.

"Good to be complete, at last!" said George Dixter, eyeing up the meal.

Maria Angelo took my arm and stood with me as we all looked down at the wonderful and quite mad feast.

"Can we all have our coffee, now?" she asked, hugging my arm and chuckling . . .

And it was only then that I realised how central I was to their meal – and how completely they were prepared to share it or even forgo part of it. I felt overwhelmed. Maria Angelo. sensing my level of emotion as though such things were still fresh in her own experience, looked at me, gave my arm another hug, and kissed the small tear that had escaped from my right eye.

It was a new year's day I will never forget . . .

XXIV

It was already dark when we set off from Grange. That had been at least two hours ago. Now it was inky black, and the twisted labyrinth of the forest was lit only by the handmade fire torches carried by Maria Angelo, George Dixter and Don Pedro. Pedro the Pomeranian trotted along happily between the four of us, content to accompany me in the relative darkness of the torchless zone between George Dixter and Don Pedro, all of us following Maria Angelo at the head of the party. I had not made the mistake of asking why I could not have one. The loving dog seemed conscious of my relative darkness, and kept brushing my legs in reassurance.

The flames atop the wooden sticks crackled and hissed as the burning pitch, soaked into the dried mosses, flared and crackled at the darkness. It was an eerie sound and highlighted a very strange situation – the most intense one I had experienced since I met the members of Don Pedro's circle. But they had invited me to be with them, and now, having agreed, I had no choice but to follow and play my part.

I was beginning to learn – though none of them had been explicit in this – that 'my part' was to go through an undocumented process of becoming more conscious of what they did. This method of teaching only by showing ran entirely counter to the norms of spiritual training in our modern world, where volumes of books are available to aid the intellectual side of the student in every esoteric genre. Within Don Pedro's circle, there was constant intensity, total listening, because to miss something might take it, irretrievably, beyond the grasp . . .

In this circle gesture had replaced speech as the token of understanding. Where knowledge was the usual intermediary of the conveying of meaning, here there was such power of gesture that it was as though understanding were conveying itself . . .

As I walked though this dark land, so familiar in the daylight, I reflected on how my attitude to Don Pedro and his companions had changed, Where once I had believed myself to be inherently superior, now, I waited in humility for what would happen next – knowing they took more care with their actions than I had ever experienced before in any situation.

And so I maintained my silence, and stilled my thoughts.

I was lost – and completely dependent on my guides. The triangle of land between Grange, Cartmel and the salt marshes west of Flookborough is a largely empty place, dominated by large tracts of forest and small hills where the rocky terrain is quite inhospitable. The few country roads make it excellent cycling country, as I had found many years ago when we had criss-crossed this landscape in the height of summer. But now, in the darkness of a cold winter night and, undoubtedly, miles from anywhere, I had no idea where I was.

Soon, we began to climb. For perhaps half an hour, we strode, with increasingly exertion, through an upward tilted forest where there was no path – and yet Maria Angelo seemed to be able to pick out her footing so that we all trudged over ground that felt like it had been trod before. As we gained height, it was as though the forest was whispering to us – and as though the price of that communication was to travel, on foot, through the darkness.

There came a point when the very atmosphere changed – and we stopped. In the effort of the dark exertion, I had not noticed that the ground had levelled. A cold wind now blew through the blackness, as though we had reach a place that was more exposed – It felt like a forested peak.

Don Pedro rested his flaming torch against a rock while he took off his old canvas rucksack. From it he took a thick blanket, which he spread out on the ground, indicating that I should rest on it, seated cross-legged, with my hands open, palms upwards. He knelt down next to me and said, "Things built on other things. Most important find first things..."

George Dixter joined him and pressed a metal object into my hand, saying only, "Later..."

Finally, Maria Angelo came forward and dropped what felt like a coin into my other, open palm. "The only path worth having," she said softly, with a hint of sadness. At that, Pedro came to curl around me several times before standing to one side, expectantly. He had been here before, I knew.

After that, things happened only in a remembered blur.

The three of them came to stand around me in a triangle, with their torches hissing over my head. Then they pulled the torches apart, stepping backwards until I could only sense their lights at the very edge of the clearing. And then the forest went completely black, with only the faint light of the stars and the full moon to decorate the ink wash.

I waited for something else to happen. I waited for what seemed an eternity before shifting my weight to relieve the stiffness. Despite the thick blanket, the cold of the ground was seeping into my body and I had to acknowledge that I did not know what to do...

Apart from the sound of the wind in the trees, there was stillness. I felt like the most alone man in the world. For a moment, anger flared in me – who the hell did they think I was to be played like this? But I knew that voice, knew its origin in the twisted fears of the early things. Faced with this knowing it subsided, to be replaced by the warm memories of the total care they had always taken of my wellbeing, and how they constantly nurtured my consciousness of what they were, what they did...

After what must have been an hour, and now shivering with the cold, I realised that I was alone. They had insisted that I leave my mobile phone behind before setting off, so there was no technology to help me. I shuffled to a kneeling position and used my fingers to examine the objects that still rested in my hands, though they were now curled against the winter cold. The one that had felt like a thick coin had two different faces. One felt like glass, or plastic; the other was metallic. It had a protrusion at one end of the curved surface that formed its narrow, circular edge. In the darkness I could do nothing else with it.

I turned my attention to the other. It was an oblong of metal. I detected a familiar smell as my fingers played with it. With a smile, I realised what it was. My fingers flew over its surfaces, eager to grasp at the familiar, and I found the hidden join with my nail, flipping open the cover of the Zippo petrol lighter. I found the primitive striking wheel and a single spark flared in the clearing. I did it again and the wick caught the spark and produced sustained light in the darkness. I stared at the flame, delighting in it and the smell of the petrol fumes, as though greeting a long, lost brother. But, with a perverse twist that is so typical of the human psyche, the light also brought me a sense of panic – the fuel in this type of lighter might not last long, and it was my only ammunition against the darkness. I considered that sentiment – 'ammunition'. My mind had said, mechanically, as though this had become a war. There, before me, were all the foundations of my ego's life. I willed myself beyond them and looked at the sheer beauty of the flame, burning steadily before me, changing the darkness in an action that was eternal, that could never be reversed.

Reason returned in good time, displacing the oneness with the flame. It had a job to do, too. My survival was also key to the exercise. It was little use been somewhat enlightened and dead – not when there was Work to do in the world . . .

I had to make good use of this gift, if I were not to die of exposure up here. I knew there was no chance of finding my way back alone and in the darkness. I had to use my wits and these gifts to survive.

I held up the lighter flame and the clearing came, faintly, into view, and with it, off to my right, the image of a modern mountain tent, framed in its bright orange fabric. I gathered my meagre possessions, rolled them into the blanket and walked over to it, closing the lighter's lid and relying on my memory of where the tent lay. With care I crossed the distance, finding the outline of the tent with my fingers. It had a zip flap and soon, I was entering it, gratefully.

Once inside, I risked using the Zippo again. The interior came into focus. There was a sleeping bag, which, in concert with the blanket, would provide all I needed; I could sleep in my clothes for warmth, tucked, safely, in its folds. The tent would insulate against the wind. There was a large rucksack in the far corner of the interior. I pulled it into the lighted zone and unfastened it. Inside were a bag of dry kindling and the tartan flask. I chuckled, knowing that the latter would contain hot coffee. They were so precise! One side pocket of the backpack contained a bottle of water, the other contained a small axe.

I poured myself a grateful cup of the hot coffee with one hand, then closed the lighter and took stock of my situation. I had no food, but a short fast would do me no harm. I had liquids and warmth. With surprise I realised I was still afraid? Of what, I wondered? In the darkness the answer came with the question: this was a new world – their 'gesture' of bringing me up here, face to face with the core elements of my life, had tipped me into a new world – their world. Even as I considered the thought, I realised that the objects of safety – the water, rucksack and even the tent, itself, were taking me away from that world, just as I had entered it . . . they would have known this, I mused, letting my hands rove over the contents of the bag. There must be something else I could do?

The Wolf with the fire was alone on the hilltop. He added

log after log to stoke it, enjoying the primeval feel of self-made heat on skin. The world would always be at his back in the darkness, but he had the power of turning; and in that power all could be brought before him. Sipping the last of the coffee, he smiled at their wisdom – and their uncompromising intent. As he retired to the warmth of the orange shelter, he noticed that the mysterious circular object, given by Maria Angeles, had fallen from the blanket on his entry. He picked it up and held it in the flickering light of the fire.

It was a compass. The dawn would see a Wolf with a way home, although the hilltop would forever be home, too. The Wolf would carry a large rucksack, within which would be every trace of his visit, packed away. A few carefully scattered ashes would be the only visible signs of his visit.

The forest would smile at his departure, wishing him a speedy return . . .

XXV

It was exactly a week after my overnight encounter with the mountain forest. The rhythm of our previous meetings drew me back to Grange and I was smiling as I parked the car and walked, excitedly, up the steep main street and towards the Sunrise Café. There were never invites of a usual nature in Don Pedro's circle, you simply had to learn to 'feel' when the time was right . . .

The place was still closed for its January break, as I knew it would be. But, sitting outside, wrapped snugly in a thick, quilted coat, was Maria Angelo. Before her on the weatherbeaten outdoor table, was a large thermos flask, much more modern than Don Pedro's.

"You survived then?" It wasn't really a question, I was sure they had monitored my return, in their own private ways. She unscrewed the outer cup of the flask, revealing a smaller one, beneath, like a set of Russian Dolls. "And what did you learn?"

She made no further move with the coffee, though her eyes danced and teased. I was going to have to sing for my breakfast. I sat back on the damp bench, equally protected in my long coat, and thought about how I might use this unexpected and frank exchange.

"I learned that fear and belonging are at the heart of what we are . . ."

"Anything else?"

I thought for a minute before replying. So many revelations had rushed through my heart and mind that night, a mere week ago.

"I learned the power and the beauty of being alive, truly alive, in a dramatic moment, one where the dangers were real and something inside was silenced."

Her smile broadened and she poured us some coffee.

"And what do we do with fear and belonging?" she asked, sipping hot coffee as the steam rose over her lower face.

I had a response to this, but it was in the form of a collection of ideas. It seemed that this unexpectedly normal meeting was there to help me clarify those and give them a form to which I could later refer. She waited, in perfect silence, while I sipped coffee and gathered my thoughts. This was one of the things I had learned early in my contact with their circle – that there was never any rush for the right response. The 'normal' chattering ways of the world were pushed aside by Don Pedro's group. In many ways their teaching could be encapsulated in the words: challenge and response, where the space for the response could be stretched out for hours, or even days . . .

"Belonging is easier", I said, putting down my cup and stretching my fingers out on the table. "Not easier in the sense of being it, but easier in the sense of how to respond to it. We need to belong, but we sacrifice so much to belong to the mundane, to the familiar. There is a sense of inner belonging that you people know and live in . . . and now I share that."

Her smile lit up her face. I think she would have graced me with one of her little kisses, had I been closer; but the table prevented it. "And fear . . .?" she asked.

"Fear is more difficult." I thought deeply about how to express what I had glimpsed up there, alone and in the darkness. "Fear is the ongoing shock of our untainted being in the world, its reaction to the unknown and that which might hurt us. But, most of the time, we are afraid of fear itself, which is crazy and takes all our energy . . ."

She looked at me and her eyes probed my soul. "And what do we do with this fear?"

The loving eyes had given me the impetus I needed. I

knew what I wanted to say. "We cannot be completely free of it, but we can bring something to sit with it, to watch it from within, to make it reveal its inner structure."

"And what is that something to sit with it? Her eyes danced, again.

"Well, in my case, it's a wolf" I said, softly.

The smile persisted as she finished her coffee. Then, she stood and came round to my side of the table and waited for me to do the same. When the restored flask was tucked into her shoulder bag, she bent to kiss the top of my head.

"I named you well," she whispered.

XXVI

The invite had been brief but specific. A time and a set of two letters and six numbers written on a card – nothing else, except that the card's hand-written lettering looked slightly smudged, as though water had been spilled on it. In a world where nothing was accidental, it might be important, or, knowing them, it might be humour . . .

Fortunately, I knew the format of the Ordnance Survey's map grid system and quickly found the place on the local walker's map. Surprisingly, it was quite close to where we lived. Knowing the terrain, I put on my walking jacket and strong boots, and left on foot.

There was no-one there when I arrived. I stood on the sunken limestone plateau, hidden from the road by the dense forest, and scanned the level surface which forms an entrance to the local gorge and white water descent – popular, in the Summertime, with canoeists. The limestone here is permanently wet from the spray of the turgid river and makes a treacherous walking surface.

Knowing that time was a relative thing within . Don Pedro's circle, I waited and simply became present to the now, expecting nothing, making no judgements and resisting the mind's urge to see the present through the lenses of the past – the hardest thing of all.

The first I knew of their arrival was when the golden fur of Pedro the Pomeranian brushed around my ankles. He hadn't made his usual "Oiff" sound, as though respecting my meditative state. I stood deliberately still, feeling for the edge of the now, the point of interaction between expectation and the truth, and letting Don Pedro enter this arena in his own way.

The voice came from behind me.

"Good!" it said, softly. "Strong presence."

Nothing more. There was an unspoken prompt in the voice behind me that contained the thought that the exercise would be better if I continued to look at the river and just listened. It was such a simple thing, but one we seldom encounter in our lives. I was in a rocky woodland glade, by a fast-flowing river, with a warm and golden animal around my ankles and simply listening to an apparently discarnate, calm voice.

"You see flow pass you?" the voice asked, gently.

I nodded, not wanting to break the spell. I looked at the churning green and white water, boiling its way down the chasm of algae-darkened white rock.

"River like time," continued the voice. "Flow must be seen in many ways to get whole picture . . ."

I could hear the mirth in his mind before he spoke again. "You could jump in – though cold today!" The chuckle was pure Don Pedro at his most mischievous. "Perhaps Summer we come back?"

I smiled but said nothing. The whole situation had a flow of its own and I did not want to be the one that broke that.

"Cold man in water," he continued. "What he see?"

I thought about it carefully. I didn't want to give the same kind of answer I would have given a year ago. I let the inner moment take the words, gently shepherding them before they solidified in my mind, removing all sense of judgement. Even if they emerged sounding naive and stupid, it didn't matter; they would be nearer to the truth that way.

"He would see the immediate churning, but he would be a part of that. Mostly he would see the high contrast of river bank moving past him – even though it would be himself that was moving, not the bank."

There was a silence then, as if my very words contained a calibration of how well I was beginning to see the world they lived in – a world now partly shared, after the vivid experience on the forested hilltop.

"So, we only see what changes?" I added, grasping my realisation.

"Yes." The gruff voice was approving, but said nothing more.

"Infinite unchanging not seen . . . yet." He just let the words hang in the air.

Then I heard a crack and part of an old branch flew past my right ear to land in the flow of the river. I watched it become part of that liquid medium and be carried past me. There came another crack and a second, identical twig narrowly missed me and landed in the churning waters. Now I could see both the first and the second. These were followed by twigs three and four, at the same intervals, with the first being just visible, now downstream, headed for the white water where the river dropped a man's height in a hundred metres.

"Marks in the water – just objects superimposed on something much more real . . . time?" I whispered.

It must have been a good response. Pedro uncoiled himself from my sheltered shins and I heard footsteps departing behind me. I knew that it was important to stay silent and aware, to let the encounter end in a way that would digest the experience.

Some time later, I climbed the path back to the narrow road. The experience had raised as many questions as it had answered, but I was smiling . . .

XXVII

It was freezing at Jenny Brown's Point, but the emailed invite had been specific: 'Come to a beach party . . .' Thankfully, it hadn't mentioned sea-bathing. When I arrived late on that Sunday afternoon, the three of them were already on the beach, playing like children. I could hear their fun long before I saw them down below. I climbed over the stile in the winding lane, then scrambled down the muddy path dotted with large limestone boulders, before coming to the uncertain edge where you can see the whole of the beach below.

The coast between Arnside and Silverdale is dotted with small coves. They are scenic and often very beautiful – but not in a classic sense. They are also a haven for wildlife. Migrating flocks of birds arrive and depart from the marshy landscape with regularity. Mud and sand vie with each other to dominate the landscape, and the beaches are crossed with watery swirls which mark the paths of streams and small rivers making their way across the sands and into Morecambe Bay in channels that constantly change. The area is fascinating but deadly. People die out there as the shifting subterranean streams change sand and turn mud into quicksand.

It is not a place for the faint-hearted.

It was next to one of these swirls of water that I located them. Their voices were carrying a long way in the fading light. Out across the vast sands, the pale winter sun was nearing the edge of the world, and cast a ghostly brightness about the edges of their darting figures. They seemed to be racing to finish something.

Eager not to be left out of the fun, I scrambled down the mud and rocks and onto the beach. I had to follow the curve of the channel to get to them. Maria Angeles had a sturdy branch in her hand. She was being guided by Don Pedro and George Dixter. A few metres away were the remains of a picnic. Had I got the time wrong? I though back to the message which had been very clear. No, I was here as invited.

I watched my mind race to the conclusion that I had been deliberately left out. It moved too quickly to stop, but I watched its flight across the darkening dome of my emotional mind as Maria Angelo put down the stick and came to give me a hug. I returned its warmth and looked up at the other two, seeing in their eyes the feeling precision that they all shared, and that I had, at least, started to appreciate. There was no implication of exclusion. I had simply arrived here when they had finished their earlier business . . . Not always about you, my correcting mind said, not always about you . . .

As I wrestled with this, the fragility of being at the centre of something when we could live elsewhere in its landscape – could live in all of its landscape, centreless – They urged me to look down at what Maria Angelo had just finished drawing.

The triangle was huge. Its vertical point faced the distance setting sun, ending in the quietly swirling waters of the channel. She pointed to the sunset to make sure I had seen the alignment.

"Yours to finish," she said, giving me the stick.

I looked down. The triangle was all of fifty metres across. "Sun setting," Don Pedro said softly. "Act, now, don't think . . ."

I took in the fading sun, the swirling stream quietly mocking me. Then I moved, running to the vertical point on the very edge of the water and digging the point of the stick deeply into the wet sand to mark the start point. With all my strength, I dragged it along the best circular arc I could manage until it joined the next point of the triangle. I couldn't believe the effort it took to cut, constantly, through the heavy sand and mud. My breathing was laboured as I began the second arc. By the time that was done I was sweating into my clothes. The third leg finished the circle, which now enclosed the triangle.

I turned to look at them. They were smiling at my exertions. I could taste the implied change in the salty air. I had become the active force, they had given me the 'tool' to carry out the task. Don Pedro nodded to me. "Ten minutes light left," he shouted, across the huge circle. I stared at my construction, cursing my lack of foresight – I had not marked the six points of what they called the Hexaflow, six points that marked the path of intelligence in the way things could happen, as the human mind reached for its potential in any manifest situation.

I ran, again, jabbing the stick into the mud, dividing each third of the circle into two more points. When I had finished, the palm of my right hand was blistered. I still had to create the hexaflow figures by joining the six points together in a pattern revealed by the division of the One of the circle by the number seven – the number of the octave, even though that is regarded as an eight, since it begins, again. On the night of the wine-filled party, Don Pedro had revealed the pattern and purpose to me on a drawing done in the earth next to his tiny caravan dwelling.

With the light dropping by the second, I ran to trace out the numbers 1-4-2-8-5-7 and back to 1 to complete the figure. I turned around, triumphant . . . but they were leaving . . .

I fought the emotion of being left out, again, but caught George Dixter's arm beckoning me to follow. As I set out after them, a blur of golden fur wrapped itself around my ankles, tripping me up on the sand. Laughing and now covered in mud, sand and a feeling of release from the self-imposed angst of ego, I stroked the friendly face, whose tongue was doing its best to remove the signs of my hard work. Together, we left the beach.

Five minutes later, the five of us were watching the darkening sandy stretch from the headland. I heard the sound of a flask being opened and turned to see Don Pedro pouring me a cup of steaming coffee from the full thermos. "Not that you cold," he chuckled.

Gratefully, I took the hot drink with dirty hands and sipped it. He pointed back to the beach. The tide was racing up the channel, flickering in the last rays of the sun, which had now flared to twice its size as it died on the horizon, to be mythically reborn after the hazardous passage through the night. Within minutes, the vast enneagram was gone, as the shallow waters of time and tide consumed it.

"But it was there, and therefore real" George Dixter said, smiling at my confusion. "And it was a damned good enneagram."

They left me contemplating the scene. It was only ten minutes later that I realised I still had Don Pedro's venerable flask cup. I smiled at the perfection of that.

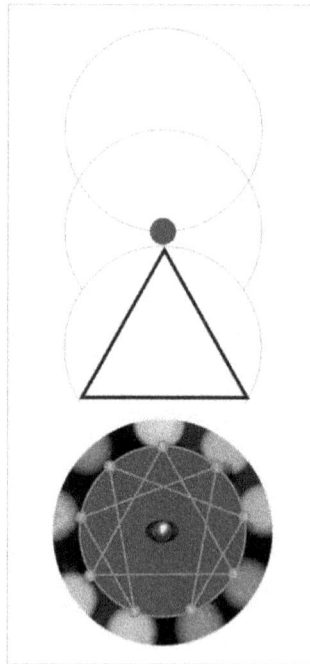

XXVIII

Everything had changed...

It had been coming for a while – about three months, in fact. That being the date we 'ordered' our new Collie pup. It had been a longstanding promise to my long-suffering wife that when we were finally settled in our Lakeland home; had demolished and rebuilt it; and decided that we were staying put, that we would have a dog...

Eleven days ago, the romantic idea had become the reality. A new four-footed young life, constantly in search of stimulation – usually oral exploration of the world – and needing so many trips to the garden and the adjacent country fields for toilet runs that we lost count. Each day we crawled into bed, quite exhausted, knowing that the little darling, good as she is, would need to be out of her basket by about six in the morning for the whole cycle to start again.

There is something fresh and wonderful about the world seen at that time of the morning. Others have written about it, too. The company of a small and warm-blooded animal is a fine way to see in the new day, even when the Lakeland weather is living up to its reputation. "That's why there are lakes, here," Don Pedro had said to me one day, when we were huddling beneath a storm under an ancient and vast golf umbrella, walking his dog, Pedro.

But the changes weren't just to our domestic life, and, now I had to face one of the consequences. With a heavy heart, I picked up the phone and rang George Dixter's number. Of the three of my companions, he was the only one with a landline.

"Hello, George?"

"What can I do for you?" his cultured voice responded with a friendly greeting.

"I have a small problem," I said, sadly.

"How small?" It was a typical Dixter response – fun, but challenging.

"About three and a quarter kilos . . ." I replied in the same ironic tone.

"Too big for a new baby then." He was laughing into the phone. "Let me guess, it's a dog!"

I should have guessed that any one of them would get it quickly. Besides, the knowledge of the new arrival would be in 'air' of our mutual presence – a phrase Don Pedro used often.

"Have you ever had a dog?' I asked, suspecting I knew the answer.

"Living on a farm? You're kidding . . . we've had several. Getting any sleep?"

"A lot less than we had planned."

He chuckled. There was something very 'easy' about Dixter. He could give you the sort of emotional space that made it easy to say what was really on your mind, regardless of how you started your sentiment.

"So, you can't join us today because you've just discovered that new Collie pups are, (a) exhausting; and (b) don't travel well?"

I held the silence, wondering if that was the full story. "Well, yes . . ."

The mental picture of me arriving in Grange, then extracting Tess from her 'crate' in the back of the car, then spending ten minutes cleaning off the doggy drool and sick with an old towel and copious wipes before trudging up the hill and while she tried to dart off in every direction before arriving . . . came to mind.

"Messy!' he said, full of good-natured understanding. "It happens . . . what will you do, instead?"

"She's okay on very short journeys, so I'll take her to the local coffee shop on the edge of Kendal, where we can watch the river. "She's never seen a river."

My wife attends adult college once a week so this would limit what could be done. Whatever I did that day, it would have to be me and Tess, alone.

"Good idea." he said, and then cut me off with, "Got to dash, talk later . . ."

An hour later, and feeling quite bereft of my regular contact with them, I sat under the winter parasol on the outside (no more warm interiors, I thought miserably) of the Costa Coffee at the edge of Kendal town centre. It was so cold and wet that Tess' excitement had turned to quiet despond and I had to pick her off the wet pavement and sit her damp and shivering body on my knee to warm her up. I had bought a large coffee before I came to rejoin her at the table; so now, at least, we could spend a few minutes looking at the river, and socialising with passing fellow dog owners. It is amazing how many people you meet when you have a dog!

A short time later, I had just drained the take-away cup when the large hand descended on my shoulder and the unmistakable gruff voice said, "Ten pounds – we pay petrol, you buy coffee!"

I turned to see Don Pedro grinning at me. Beside him George Dixter was looking at the river Kent in full flood and smiling, as though this were the most natural thing in the world.

I took out my wallet, speechless. "I, I . . ."

"Latté, then . . ." He took the offered ten pound note, and with that the bulk of our spiritual leader disappeared into the coffee shop. Dixter took a seat opposite me, under the sodden parasol and proceeded to read his paper, still silent and occasionally looking up at Tess, now warming up a little on my muddy lap. At length, Don Pedro returned, carrying three cups.

"Going to get expensive for you, meeting like this!" he laughed.

"Yes," I joined in with the humour. "Sorry about that. We didn't really foresee what an effect it would have . . ."

George Dixter looked up from his paper and took a sip of coffee, looking intently at Don Pedro, who returned his gaze.

"Still trying change what is . . . he'll never learn!" they both chortled.

XXIX

It had been a week since Don Pedro and George Dixter had driven to see me at the coffee shop in Kendal. It seemed a distant memory. The seven days had been filled with a fury of puppy duties, and I seemed to be buried in a never-ending cycle of monitoring and walks, at all times of the day and night, as Tess got through the thirteenth week of her life.

Towards the end of the week we had a breakthrough. The previous guarantee of car sickness began to abate, as long as we put her in the back seat and kept the expensive dog crate in the car boot out of the equation. We'd have settled for trotting alongside the car, to be honest, we were so relieved to think that there was light at the end of the car problem.

And so it was that, with my wife at college, once again, I decide to risk all and drive Tess and I to Grange for a walk along the sea front. It was the time of year for the very high tides, and the previous year's had been spectacular. I drove slowly, checking that she was okay in the large and floppy dog bed we had sourced from the local market in Kendal. It had a waterproof lining, so, if disaster struck, I could use the vast cleaning kit in the boot to clean things up. We were getting very used to mopping up.

Happily, she wasn't sick . . . a bit of slavering, but otherwise fine. Passing Grange station, I sighed with relief that normal-ish journeys were becoming possible. Arriving at the main car park, I made a big fuss of her and fitted the lead so we could go walking on the very deserted promenade. She didn't like the strong wind, but seemed content to be outside the car and in the fresh air.

I thought about the year that had just passed. The initial meeting with Don Pedro now seemed prophetic, as though it marked a portal that had been waiting for me. One of my favourite sources of esoteric knowledge is Gurdjieff, and he always maintained that a genuine desire to probe deeper into the spiritual life prompted a kind of response from the world – our own world. He called this response 'magnetic centre' – a reference to how the right things are attracted to the seeker in such situations. Those things may not be right for another; but they are appropriate for the person at the centre of that world.

Things had moved so quickly after that meeting. My initial impression that he terrorised Maria Angelo, the waitress at the Sunrise Café, had given way to a realisation that they were constantly involved in a 'theatre of the moment', playing out a deadly serious game of gesture and response – and all at a much deeper level of meaning than that normally engaged in by two people. There were no textbooks in Don Pedro's world; it was all teaching in the 'now'.

I considered the picture of Tess and I walking along the promenade, under the dark clouds and in the buffeting winds. I looked at Tess, all floppy and spontaneous, and wondered if Don Pedro had seen something similarly 'young' in my attempts to be superior to him on that first, cold morning?

The idea of a true self had been at the heart of everything that had happened between the four of us. It had come as a shock that what we view as ourselves is really a hierarchy of reactions, a composite 'me' that takes over selfhood from an early age. This process is, of course, necessary – without it we would never be strong and competent in the world; and yet this ego, and its undoing, is the start point for the true spiritual journey home.

We reached a point where there is an open level crossing on the Lancaster-Barrow railway line. I urged Tess though the white gate, checking carefully before we ventured onto the tracks, her tail wagging, furiously, at the new terrain.

I thought about the puppy analogy, again. It is uncomfortable to come to accept that you don't know things. It is even more uncomfortable to feel the peeling back of your worldly self in the interest of what lies beneath. That hardship, that pain, is the reason so many people chose a path filled with imagination rather than the simple truth of their own lives. There is nothing wrong with imagination used creatively; but I had found out the hard way how it is used by the ego to suppress the truly spiritual search – which must begin with honesty about oneself. My suspicion is that this can only be given by another. We cannot see ourselves, but our ego reacts when others do . . .

This, then, had been the substance of the year. And added to that, when we had gone through the early stages, had come the 'trials' of trust. To believe that we exist in a caring universe is not a popular view; and yet it is at the heart of so much of the ancient wisdom. Perhaps it is something we can only learn bit by bit.

Tess and I climbed the steep hill towards the town centre. I was quite excited at the slim possibility of seeing them again. We had made no plans, but Maria Angelo worked in the Sunrise Café and there was a chance that my adopted mentor, and fellow student, might me there.

We turned the final corner to arrive at the café.

It was closed. A small sign on the front door said they were taking advantage of the winter to re-furbish the interior. There was no indication of when it would re-open. I was about to leave, when I saw the envelope. It had become sodden by the rain. On it was the 'circle name' that Maria Angelo had given me . . . Lobo.

About the author: Steve is a well-known figure in the esoteric world and has been a keynote presenter at many conferences and workshops. Born into a Rosicrucian family in Bolton, Lancashire, in 1954, Steve grew up surrounded by mystical discussion and fascinating but often peculiar grown-ups. In adult life, and alongside a career in IT, he became an officer and then the Lodge Master of the Rosicrucian Order AMORC's John Dalton Chapter in Manchester, eventually becoming a field officer. This began an intensive period of service culminating in the role of Grand Councillor for the North of England, Scotland and Ireland.

Steve retired from AMORC in 2005 with full military honours and fond memories of some wonderful times shared, including a final initiation in the King's Chamber of the Great Pyramid of Gizeh - something not easily bettered!

Shortly after, he met Dolores Ashcroft-Nowicki, Director of Studies of the Servants of the Light School, and her husband Michael, then in charge of all the back-office systems for SOL. It was a prophetic meeting as Steve was, shortly thereafter, to create SOL's computerised administration systems for Dolores and Michael, set up a SOL Lodge in Manchester, and become a founding member of the ARC Administration team. Part of this undertaking was to be invited into SOL's House of the Amethyst and take the SOL highest initiation - the Third Degree - Adept.

In 2012, Steve became the Founding Director of the Silent Eye, a modern Mystery School, along with Sue Vincent and Stuart France.

Steve publishes a regular blog where confusion, humour and occasional teaching may be found.

stevetanham.wordpress.com

The Silent Eye

The Silent Eye School of Consciousness is a modern Mystery School that seeks to allow its students to find the inherent magic in living and being.

With students around the world the School offers a fully supervised and practical correspondence course that explores the self through guided inner journeys and daily exercises. It also offers regular workshops, open to all, that combine sacred drama, lectures and informal gatherings to bring the teachings to life in a vivid and exciting format.

The Silent Eye operates on a not-for-profit basis. Full details of the School, its methods and teachings may be found on the official website:

www.thesilenteye.co.uk

a modern mystery school

Other Books by Steve Tanham:

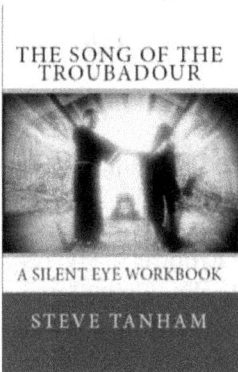

THE SONG OF THE TROUBADOUR:

A Silent Eye Workbook

Steve Tanham

Foreword by Sue Vincent

With contributions from Stuart France and those who were there to share this very special journey.

"Being is without beginning and end. This flowing, loving, intelligence is the basis of everything we know. Whatever level of consciousness we attain, it will only reveal the greater and greater depth of Being that has always been there within us and before us.

Being also forms the objects that we believe are separated from us. But the Reality and the Truth are that we live and have our own being in a sea of endless loving energy that is our true home. There is no separation, there is in the end, no journey; there is only realisation, and seeing. What unveils itself before us, was always there."

A group of pilgrims have been brought together in the ancient monastery of the Keepers of the First Flame. Unexpectedly, the door opens and into their midst stride the Troubadours, holding a Child by the hand…. a very special Child in whom the Light of Being shines clear… and who can see the world as it really is. The Troubadours are on an urgent mission to save the life of a King and they enlist the aid of the pilgrims to care for the Child as they fathom the meaning an ancient and prophetic riddle….

Thus began the inaugural weekend that saw the Birthing of the Silent Eye, a modern Mystery School. This workbook is both a practical transcript of the dramatic rituals of that weekend and the story of that Birth. The book opens a window onto the workings of a modern Mystery school, sharing the accounts of some of those who attended the weekend as well as the detailed script of the powerful ritual drama. If you have ever wondered what really goes on… this book is for you.

LAND OF THE EXILES

A Silent Eye Workbook with Practical Notes

Steve Tanham

With contributions from Sue Vincent, Stuart France and the Companions of the Hawk.

In April 2014 the Silent Eye, a modern Mystery School, hosted the Land of the Exiles as a weekend workshop. These annual gatherings attract people from across the world to share a unique approach to the spiritual journey that is taken by all. Over the course of the workshop a story unfolds, dramatic and emotive, engaging the hearts and minds of the participants, shadowing forth the challenges of the inner journey to awakening. This workbook includes the script from that journey, along with practical and explanatory notes, as well as the personal accounts of some of the Companions who shared an epic journey of the imagination as a spaceship crash-lands on a far-flung planet, and a cyborg forces them to play out the story of the ancient gods of Egypt, intent of calculating just what it means to be human...

A practical guide to a fully scripted ritual workshop from the Silent Eye, a modern Mystery School.

Illustrated

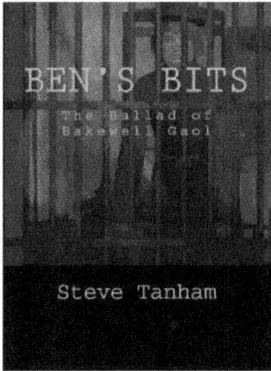

BEN'S BITS:
The Ballad of Bakewell Gaol

A Graphic Novel

Steve Tanham

"How long, now? How long have I been locked in here? One hour, maybe two? One pace, two paces, three . . . I stop at three, drowning in the exact middle of the dark space of the cell in Bakewell Gaol. They can't leave me here! Look, this is just a mistake, you don't understand, we were only..."

Ben has been arrested for his part in a scheme hatched by Wen to re-site an ancient stone in its original position. If only he had not gone back for the gun... Don and Wen are nowhere to be found and the judge seems to want an example to be made... and Ben is all he has....

Three poems written for the Lands of Exile trilogy by Stuart France and Sue Vincent, presented as a graphic novel in full colour.